POSITIVE THINKING

The Fastest Way to Build Positive Thinking

(Improve Your Life Instantly With Positive Thinking Meditation Techniques)

Lynette Green

Published By Jackson Denver

Lynette Green

All Rights Reserved

Positive Thinking: The Fastest Way to Build Positive Thinking (Improve Your Life Instantly With Positive Thinking Meditation Techniques)

ISBN 978-1-77485-269-9

All rights reserved. No part of this guide may be reproduced in any form without permission in writing from the publisher except in the case of brief quotations embodied in critical articles or reviews.

Legal & Disclaimer

The information contained in this book is not designed to replace or take the place of any form of medicine or professional medical advice. The information in this book has been provided for educational and entertainment purposes only.

The information contained in this book has been compiled from sources deemed reliable, and it is accurate to the best of the Author's knowledge; however, the Author cannot guarantee its accuracy and validity and cannot be held liable for any errors or omissions. Changes are periodically made to this book. You must consult your doctor or get professional medical advice before using any of the suggested remedies, techniques, or information in this book.

Upon using the information contained in this book, you agree to hold harmless the Author from and against any damages, costs, and expenses, including any legal fees potentially resulting from the application of any of the information provided by this guide. This disclaimer applies to any damages or injury caused by the use and application, whether directly or indirectly, of any advice or information presented, whether for breach of contract, tort, negligence, personal injury, criminal intent, or under any other cause of action.

You agree to accept all risks of using the information presented inside this book. You need to consult a professional medical practitioner in order to ensure you are both able and healthy enough to participate in this program.

Table of Contents

Introduction 1

Chapter 1: Seed of thought are the product of your thoughts 6

Chapter 2: The Effects of a Negative Mental State on your Health 16

Chapter 3: "Stop Worrying" 35

Chapter 4: Relaxing Anxiety 51

Chapter 5: The Superiority Complex and Self-Doubt 66

Chapter 6: The Habits, Rituals, and Daily Habits, Rituals & Daily 87

Chapter 7: The Effects of a negative mindset on your Quality of Life 109

Chapter 8: Think It 121

Chapter 9: Loving 128

Chapter 10: Take proper care of your body 147

Chapter 11: Establishing Fruitful Relationships 153

Chapter 12: How Thinking Positively can assist us in developing our abilities and enhancing our work performance. Enhancing Our Health 160

Chapter 13: Tips for Practical Use to Encourage You to Think Positive 177

Conclusion 183

Introduction

If you've bought this book, you're likely to need to make a major shift in your mindset. This is a normal thing to experience in the life of a person when they discover there are some shortcomings in their lives which they are not happy about. A change in mindset could bring about other positive life changes.

This is crucial for anyone who is seeking to increase the success in your life. What a person's definition of success is different between people. Some may believe that wealth is the only definition of success, while others might think that building solid relationships is the essence of success.

The mindset of a person is crucial in their personal, professional and romantic lives. If you don't have a positive and positive mindset, it's easy to be a victim of negative thoughts and bad behaviors like procrastination. There are many things that you must change and master in your daily life to improve your mental outlook. This means changing your thoughts about success, how you think about success and being conscious.

Oft times, the constant comparisons we make of ourselves with the elite 1% of people is damaging to our mental outlook. The environment we were raised in and the time we spent growing up contribute significantly to the way our mental outlook is to this day. If someone grew up in a strict, strict family that did not give any recognition to their position to them or were always dragged down by a sibling , or if they grew in a home with parents who were not involved and were constantly dependent on others and their own needs, this could negatively impact their mental outlook in the future.

Studies have shown that children who were raised in families that did not provide them with enough love often showed a negative attitude as compared to children who were raised in families that displayed more affection.

These are the reasons why being positive and having a functional mental state is vital in the present. Today individuals must constantly keep in mind the achievements they have accomplished, regardless of how significant or small it might be.

It is essential for people to be constantly working on self-esteem and related factors to live a balanced lifestyle. A person's attitude and how they perceive themselves are the most significant factor in the vital process of making a decision.

When you are in a state of health it is possible to notice changes not just yourself, but also influence other aspects of your life, such as family friends, friendships, and relationships. If your mental health is positive and positive, it will eventually improve your self-confidence which is essential to developing your career and improving relationships with those you meet in your daily life.

Before you begin reading this book, begin thinking about what areas in your life you'd prefer to make changes to. Are you trying to make your life more professional? Are you looking to be promoted? Earn a raise? Do you want for people to make romantic relationships with? No matter what the attitude you require is similar.

This book I'll be teaching you about various subjects in relation to how you can shift your perspective to one that is more healthy and more positive. I'll begin by explaining the fundamentals of mind and also the negative effects of having a negative mental attitude. Understanding the long-term and health consequences of having a negative attitude will enable you to see the importance of use a positive mental attitude. I will then educate you how an optimistic mindset can positively impact your life.

In the middle of the book, I'll teach you how to evaluate your own inner self. This covers areas such as your self-esteem, self-criticism, and self-control. These areas are essential as the person's mental state is constructed by their self-esteem, self-criticism, and self-control.

If you are able to learn more about these subjects and understanding what your views and beliefs are derived from. In this book, I'll teach you how to alter your perspective employing a variety of methods. I will guide you through a standard method known as Cognitive Behavioral Therapy (CBT) followed by another method that is more relaxed that is mindful and meditation.

I'll also provide you with workout sheets and the habits you'll must focus on to improve your general mindset.

Chapter 1: Seed of thought are the product of your thoughts

"With every second of anger, you've lost more than 60 seconds of joy."

What you say, what do, and how you feel - all is a result of your thoughts It all begins with one thought.

Thoughts are just like seeds. Every one one of that will produce fruit that will give you a distinct taste. Thinking can bring destructive or creative and hatred or love acceptance or resentment. If we can understand and master the ability to regulate our thought patterns we will feel peace, joy and security within our hearts. Positive thinking can teach us how to behave instead of reacting "guide" our lives rather than letting behaviour of others, our past experiences, or the present situation influence our thoughts.

Have you stopped to take a closer look at the images in your mind , and the thoughts that you think about? Based on calculations that the average person is able to have between 30,000 and 50,000 thoughts every day. An anxious mind generates more thoughts, as high as 80000 thoughts. It is likely that you've been in a state anxious tension due to an unexpected event that has occurred in your life. you've got a lot of thoughts running through your head.

The mind is a powerful capacity to work continuously, even while we sleep. It is said that thought is the basis for all the actions and feelings. Therefore, by forming positive and healthy mental images, we are able to activate our potential for positive change.

Your life is a summation that you have made (including the conscious and unconscious). If you influence your choice process, you will be able to take control of all aspects that you live in. It is possible to achieve freedom by taking responsibility for your life. The power of thought is the mind. "Our attitudes towards things outside is determined by our way of thinking within ourselves." Park Cousins - Food that can fuel our bodies. If you plan to race a marathon, you'll need to eat lots of protein and energy-rich meals to be able to cover long distances. In contrast If your body is exposed to harmful foods, you might suffer stomach pains and feel tired and lethargic. Similar to that thinking fuels your mind. If you're having negative, useless , and unproductive thoughts, they'll take away the vitality of the mind. If you think positively you "energize" you mind providing you with the power and determination to take on the problems and problems of daily life. According to research in the field of medicine around 75% to 90percent of all physical diseases stem from our minds and begin from our thought patterns. In simple terms what you put into your mind influence your health. Are our bodies affected when we're upset or stressed? In tension, the muscle around the eyes blocks blood flow and creates pressure points that are uncomfortable to the human body. Shoulder pain, neck pain and headaches are usually due to stress or negative thoughts. However the moment we think positive and calm thoughts in our minds muscles relax, oxygen levels decrease, blood pressure falls and the rate of heart disease decreases dramatically. Half an hour Research on Science enjoying life (The Association for Research into the Science of Enjoyment ARISE) ARISE) has proven the relationship between the emotions of humans for chemical reactions that happen within the body. When people experience positive thoughts and feel a sense of happiness, their body produces an abundance of antibodies, which help protect your body against respiratory illnesses. They also produce natural painkillers that are believed to combat cancer , counteract the negative effects caused by "stress" and help to make the surrounding area positive energy. However in the event that they experience negative thoughts and are unhappy their bodies react to the situation by reducing immunity, which causes the body to operate in a state of stagnation and an increased risk of developing disease. . Our thoughts and our relationships "Take very good care of you thoughts and pay attention to it and you'll be your own best friends. Whatever your location or what language you speak and what language you speak, I will always be my friend or enemy. You can chooseto be either your friendliest or most feared adversary . " BK Dadi Jaki As stated as a thought process, it is the first step to create thoughts, words and actions. It is therefore important to manage your thoughts. This helps you control your emotions as well as actions, and words. We have seen in the previous section that thought can have a significant impact on our body. It is an aspect that influences the environment that we are in as well as our interactions with the people who surround us. Positive thinking can lead to harmonious relationships whereas negative thoughts can cause conflict and discord among those in their vicinity. When we are thinking negatively about others, it can decrease our tolerance levels and the tension in relationships will increase and escalate. A time when I knew that I can only influence others, but be unable to "control" them I would experience an elation. I can't control other people, but I can master my response to other people. People may behave badly however I do have the option of how I react to their actions. This means that, even though there are times when we feel "negative" in our surroundings it is possible to be positive. We spend the majority the time "reacting" to others' actions to anger, boredom or anger when they behave in a manner we prefer. If we are able accept their opinions and keep the attention of their positive points, we'll be content whenever they're around; while at the same time, it could influence the people around us. This way, we start to recognize being the authors of our thoughts. If we think of positive, peaceful, and happy thoughts, they impact others who surround us. It is an easy method to share your happiness with other people. Similar to throwing stones into the water it will cause ripples and produce waves. Figure 2 illustrates the negative results of negative thoughts "I dislike my coworker". These thoughts have a huge impact on our lives. The average person spends 8 hours each day working when negative thoughts about our colleagues fill our thoughts, we'll be forced to endure 8 hours of gruelling or miserable work. Thinking negative thoughts about negative people is a way to make us feel worse for us. If you switch negative thoughts to positive thoughts about your workplace and your colleagues, you'll be more relaxed. The same can be said on our personal relationships. Five major types of thinking The five kinds of thinking positive thinking. This kind of thinking is beneficial to us as well as others. It's being positive, accepting , and compassionate mindset ... for instance looking at half the glass of water you'll notice "half an ounce of water" instead of "half an empty glass of water" which means you need to be focused on what you have and be content with it, rather than being discontent with what you don't have. The image of a half glass of water can be an image that represents various things that happen that happen in our lives. For instance, when we take a look at other people instead of dwelling on their flaws and shortcomings, which we tend to tend to do, positive thinking will allow us to focus on our strengths and strengths. Their good qualities. There's a wonderful expression, "Eat whatever you eat" This means we develop into what we maintain in our minds. By keeping the positive aspects of others in our consciousness and allowing our thoughts to "eat" positive thoughts can help the good qualities grow within us. Also in bringing others' weaknesses and shortcomings into our minds and accept them as a reality, they increase the weaknesses within us. Thus, positive thinking can bring you a lot of happiness throughout your life. Negative thinking: A type of thinking that's detrimental to yourself and others. These are thoughts that cause you to be anger, narrow-minded, causing pain to your self or others, or judging ... Negative thoughts The thought of thinking about the past or thoughts beyond your control of. Control yourself by thinking: "Why? ", "If only" ... which includes suspicion guilt, regret worrying about minor items ... Need to think about how to organize your day: " I need to meet him right now", "I have to get to the place" ... Thinking from the top of the list: Thinking in terms of the qualities, values and values of an individual or a human being like peace, kindness and collaboration etc.These are the thoughts that are connected to understanding the purpose of our lives, or the things that are happening in the world around us. The forward-thinking process is not only dependent on the immediate reality but also the consequences of our actions. Thinking forward can help us develop an outlook that is not selfish but in the interest of all. It is possible to focus our thoughts to wake them up within our minds. The upward thoughts accumulate gradually through understanding the spirituality of life, pondering the significance of things, and watching our actions. Positive thinking can give us a feeling of happiness and a vivacious life. If we have a positive outlook you will become an energy source for our own lives. Conversely the negative can drain the internal energy and energy within, making us feel totally empty. The result of the feeling of emptyness is stress and anxiety. If we're not able to be positive this can result in depression. Today depression is rising for both old and young. If someone is negative, they can make themselves fearful as well as others surrounding them. It is important to ask the question "What type of feeling do I really desire?". The majority of us will say that we desire peace. If we have positive thoughts and speak with confidence, your words are uplifting and our actions will be successful and everything will be fine.

Chapter 2: The Effects of a Negative Mental State on your Health

People often associate negativity with those who suffer from personality disorders such as narcissists or sociopaths. But this isn't the case. It is not the same thing. Oxford Dictionary definition for negativity says "the form of expression that expresses criticism or a negative view of something."

While a narcissist might appear negative because of the way they deal with the victims they hurt, their attitude isn't necessarily negative. They actually have an overinflated self-image about themselves. Negativity is a mentality which people are prone to and that affects their behavior and emotions.

It is possible to see negativity in those who have recently suffered a trauma, like divorce. One who was confident and optimistic about their future could be sceptical and doubt the possibility of ever finding happiness ever again.

It is possible to spot negative thoughts in someone struggling with depression. Because of the imbalance in the brain's chemicals that cause depression, they don't have the capacity to be positive. People who are depressed may be completely unsure regarding their future and it could get to the point that they're unable to get up to take care of their daily requirements.

Negativity manifests in different ways for each individual. Some individuals develop an unhappiness due to an event which has occurred to them, while others may be suffering from a negative mental state because of your mental state.

If you believe you're one who suffers with a negative attitude for some time it is essential to determine the reason is that you are suffering from one. Perhaps something tragic occurred to you recently? Do you think that it's related to mental health?

Fortunately, negative thinking is able to be transformed since your brain can be a flexible organ. Through the correct coaching treatment, therapy, and routine the person can change their brain's wiring to produce more positive thoughts , as opposed those that are negative. Thoughts that are negative can come from numerous places.

As we've said, negative thoughts may be the result of poor mental health. They can also be a result of self-esteem issues in which your mental state is made from the words of others who have spoken to you in the past negatively. It could also be the result of trauma and negative thoughts are stored in your brain to safeguard you from the possibility of the same thing repeated.

Positive thoughts are able to be eliminated and replaced with positive ones with the proper training. Except for severe mental illness such as chronic depression, when medications will be administered to alleviate the symptoms. That's why finding out what is causing your negative mood is crucial. If your negativity stems from a mental disorder that has a long-term history It is essential to be diagnosed by medical professionals so they can determine if you require medication or not.

In the event that your stress stems from an event that you have experienced and you are feeling low about yourself, therapy as well as positive exercises can assist you in rewiring your mind.

Long-Term Impacts

Poor mental health is one of the most prevalent places where negative thoughts stem from. However, it can also be the root of an unhappiness mindset. Today, in the world of modern times millions of people suffer from illnesses like anxiety and depression. They frequently find themselves stricken with thoughts of negativity.

The next chapter I'll be educating you on the long-term effects associated with having a negative attitude. In this chapter, we will take an examination of anxiety and depression as well as their causes and the signs and symptoms. There's a lot of research to be conducted in the area of whether negative mental attitudes cause mental health problems and if health problems can cause negative thinking.

No matter what the reason the fact is that both can cause someone to feel very negative. If you have a diagnosis of one of these mental disorders then you'll need to consult an expert in health care to determine the cause and find the right treatment. Let's examine depression first.

Depression

The definition of depression in the dictionary is "severe depressing feelings and despair. But it is important to be aware not to confuse depression with feelings of grief or sadness. The loss of a loved one or the breaking up of a relationship are extremely difficult that a person has to go through and endure.

When you are going through a difficult time it is normal to feel sadness and sorrow to manifest as a reaction to these events. Anyone who is experiencing losses or events may often refer to themselves as depressed.'

However sadness isn't an indication of having a depression disorder. The grieving process of a person is distinct for every person however, it shares many of the experiences that a depression condition can bring. Depression and grief-related feelings trigger feelings of sadness as well as withdrawal from routine life.

Here are a few ways to explain the reasons they are different

When someone is feeling feelings of grief, these pain can come in waves. They're usually mixed with positive memories of the person who passed away. If someone is experiencing profound grief, their enthusiasm and mood decreases for about two weeks.

If someone is in sadness, their self-esteem doesn't change too in any way. If someone is depressed is a constant feeling of self-loathing and utter lack of worthiness.

For the majority of people, the loss of a beloved one can trigger major depression. For others, it could mean losing their job, or being an assault victim. If depression and grief occur together, the grief tends to be the most severe and is more prolonged than grief that does not have depression. There's some similarities between grief and depression however the fact that they're not identical, they're still distinct. The ability to help a person differentiate between depression and grief is essential for them to receive help, support, or even treatment.

The signs of depression

If you know which signs are related to depression, it will aid in determining the difference between a time of grief to a real depression disorder. If someone is feeling down, has negative thoughts, or is having difficulty sleeping, it doesn't necessarily mean they suffer from depression. To be able to be diagnosed as having a depression disorder it is necessary to show the following signs:

The person's symptoms have to be completely new or appear to be significantly more severe compared to the way they behaved prior to the depression episode.

The patient's symptoms should last throughout the day, and must be as regular as they are over at minimum two weeks consecutively.

The episode the person experiences should also be accompanied by impairment in functioning or severe clinical distress.

The most frequent signs of depression are emotional symptoms. These are the symptoms which you feel are negatively the state of your mind is affecting you.

Here are a few examples of few of the emotional symptoms sufferers of depression be able to endure:

The constant sadness refers to the sadness which occurs in people who are depressed with no reason. The feeling can be extremely intenseand often it feels like there is nothing that can help it to disappear.

Feeling of being unworthy Feeling of worthlessness: People who are depressed can experience unreal feelings of inadequacy or guilt. There is usually no specific incident that triggers these feelings. They just happen randomly.

Negative, suicidal or dark thoughts: These kinds of thoughts may occur often during depression. These thoughts should be considered seriously and if a person experiences these feelings should seek immediate help.

A loss of interest or enjoyment in pursuits that you previously enjoyed by a person who is depressed might suffer from a lack of interest that can affect all aspects of their lives. This could range from not being able to find enjoyment in the previous activities to daily activities that they was previously able to enjoy.

Anxiety

The standard description of anxiety is "feeling of anxiety, nervousness or unease. This definition may appear to sound much better than it actually is. Most times the anxiety is accompanied by other grave issues, such as anxiety attacks or extreme anxiety.

Did you consider an anxiety disorder is among the most commonly diagnosed mental disorders across the United States presently? The number of people suffering from anxiety disorders is currently the lives of 40 million Americans, or about 18% of population. This is not a tiny number.

In the past, humans have been experiencing anxiety since the time of barbarism. At the time anxiety was extremely useful to shield us from potentially dangerous situations. Anxiety is a fundamental emotion, and it is a feeling that virtually every animal species experiences. It triggers an instinctive fight-or-flight response.

In the present anxiety is now a major issue, and instead of helping us to survive and thrive, it's actually causing problems for many people's lives.

Anxiety is an essential emotion that all animals feel. It's not a pleasant sensation or experience however, it isn't harmful to us. In reality, anxiety is an extremely beneficial experience for most living creatures in certain circumstances. It triggers our highly-needed combat or flight reaction.

While in our modern society there is no longer the desire to fighting or fleeing, the instinct remains ingrained in us and it's impossible to eradicate it from our natural instincts. Many people want to eliminate all anxiety However, a goal like this isn't feasible or even realistic. Instead, those suffering from anxiety need to learn to redirect it in a way that is beneficial, not becoming debilitating.

When we know the causes of anxiety the definition of anxiety, we will be able to use appropriate strategies to manage anxiety. Based on the assumption the fact that we all experience anxiety as a natural reaction when we feel threatened; If a person believes they're being threatened and is in danger, their fight or flight response triggers.

If the instinct to fight is activated the mind has one major goal that is to defend itself by fleeing, or fighting the perceived threat. The person in danger transmits a signal to the autonomic nervous system that causes it to respond to release adrenalin and noradrenalin in their mind. When the threat that they perceive is gone our nervous systems start to block these chemicals and destroy the substances in order to calm the body back.

Signs of anxiety

People who suffer from anxiety may not be aware that it's the reason. Because a majority of anxiety-related symptoms are physical, the majority of people believe they are suffering from an illness that is medical. Most of the time anxiety symptoms can be controlled or controlled with basic over-the-counter drugs however, sometimes it is necessary to determine the root of the issue to ease the symptoms.

If your anxiety grows beyond the triggers that caused it and they start to affect your daily life. This can result in an anxiety disorder. When you are aware of the symptoms of anxiety it is possible to determine what assistance you require. Here are the most frequent signs of anxiety

Frequent Stress

Excessive Agitation

Reluctance

Fatigue

Trouble with Concentration

Irritability

Tensed Muscles

Insomnia

Panic Attacks

Beware of Certain Situations

Irrational Fears

Weight Loss/Gain

Compulsive behavior

Addictions

Stress

A lot of experts from around the world are all in agreement that the idea that stress is just a psychological experience is a dangerous idea. They employed an analogy to further explain this. Because humans' stress-related response changed over the course of thousands over the years, this first aids our ancestors in identifying dangers and foods.

It's natural. Without it, we might be moving to woo bears, rather than harvesting fruits from the forests. There were a variety of dangers in the past which range from avoiding predators to locating food. It's all natural as is our response to stress we wouldn't have been able to get this far.

But, what's not typical is the way modern living exposes us to more subtle dangers, yet the stress that we experience is never-ending. It is because we are overloaded with stimulation, having to manage multiple tasks and always in motion. In simpler terms, human beings are not designed to be able to run from predators for more than 10 hours every day without breaks. This is, in essence, the way humans operate in the modern world.

Many experts have described the condition that is common to chronic stress that we face as "super tension." We are currently constantly stricken by stresses that we often think of as commonplace. This can include: inadequate wages and job satisfaction, feeling stressed and not enough time to spend with friends and family as well as a lack of time for outdoor activities or in the noise, as well as feeling that their lives have no purpose or significance.

The most bizarre aspect the above is our bodies can't physically discern the difference between being attacked by a bear or having a bad job assessment. The physiological and chemical reaction in our bodies is exactly the identical. Because of this, the body starts to become tired because of the severity of the strain.

If people are being stressed throughout the day, they're overusing every aspect within their own body. The result is a plethora of stress-related symptoms. Indeed, for some, stress levels can be so high that it goes from irritating to becoming an affliction that is debilitating. There are many people who develop mental disorders when in a stressful situation for example, depression and anxiety. Let's look at the changes that occur in our biochemistry when we're stressed.

The signs of stress

Stress manifests differently, based on the person however, there are a few commonly observed symptoms that all sufferers experience. When you know the symptoms that are that are associated with stress, you'll be able recognize the signs you're experiencing stress.

One of the most important aspects of managing stress is identifying the stressors and triggers. In order to to manage stress it is essential to understand the symptoms you display when you're stressed, and determine what triggers cause them. Let's examine the most commonly observed signs of stress:

* Acne

* Headaches

* Chronic Pain

* Frequent Sickness

* Sleepiness and Decreased Energy

* Libido Decrease

* Digestive Issues

* Appetite Changes

* Depression

* Rapid Heartbeat

* Sweating

We've learned that negative thoughts can impact a person's health in a negative way. This is a concern for anxiety levels as well as mental health. They are all closely connected and if one is suffering, the other are likely to suffer as well. Let's first look at what stress actually is and what the signs are.

The chapter will allow you to evaluate the extent to which your negative thoughts are impacting you. It is hard to fully be aware of the consequences of your negative thoughts until you can examine the effects in a impartial perspective. Most likely, your negative thoughts may be negatively impacting your work, health or relationships.

Chapter 3: "Stop Worrying"

We all have worries every now and then. You fret about others and yourself every day. It's normal to a degree. It is normal to be concerned about the possibility of failing or your safety or other potential factors. It's natural, since animals are required to be concerned about their food until they are able to feed themselves. But, there's some point at which worrying about food is not healthy. If you are always worrying to the point that it has taken over your life, it is time to act. You should be able to take pleasure in your life. While you might be anxious at times but it shouldn't stop you from doing your everyday activities. When worry becomes a major issue and becomes a problem, you must pay care.

You need to be able to let go of worrying. There is always a chance that something negative will happen but you need to be able to look for optimism and positivity rather than dwelling upon the possibility of something going wrong. You should be able to be present and be focused on having fun instead of dwelling on your mistakes in the past or the possibility of what might be the cause of the next problem. You should be able to live your life in the present and not spend each minute of it fretting. It's essential to stop thinking about the "what-ifs" and build the capacity to concentrate on the ideal result. There's a compromise between having a realistic outlook and remaining positive. You must be able find the right equilibrium. It is also important to be more aware of your own as well as your mood.

Stop worrying

It's not difficult to understand it's as simple as letting go of worrying. While it may seem much more complicated than it is however, you can teach your brain to worry less and be more relaxed. Stress can be reduced and you can greatly reduce the effects of worry and prevent it from happening. But, it will require lots of practice and perseverance as you advancement. If you worry naturally, it will become a habit that can take time to change with healthier routines. You should be able to alter your thinking to decrease the amount of worry you experience.

There are many ways to cut down how much time you're spending fretting. One option is to put aside some time to think. Instead of trying to suppress your worries and not addressing them until they reach a stage where they become overwhelming take time every day to allow your emotions to flow. Instead of fighting them, let yourself experience all the things. It is possible to imagine yourself reacting too much; this can allow you to appreciate the benefits (or more so) it is to let your emotions control you. Spending a few minutes each day letting your emotions out can help you. You can keep a diary or note everything down. You could write out every thought and erase it immediately afterward so that you be able to see the clearing of your thoughts before your eyes. You can choose to confide in someone whom you are comfortable with, and allow yourself to be a bit ranty for a while to let it all out. Whatever the case, it's healthy to let your emotions flow instead of trying to suppress them.

Discover the source of your issues. You might have too much free time and you simply want something to distract your thoughts. You can engage in a pastime to keep your mind active. It could be a specific occasion that causes you to worry. You might feel stressed as you browse social media sites, while you judge yourself against other people and feel like you're not enough. Maybe your concerns stem from an incident in your past that you've not yet been able to overcome. Whatever the reason it's important to take a moment to consider the reasons why you're worried and come up with an answer for the issue.

Another factor to take into consideration is whether your issues are manageable or not. If your concern has a solution, you should come up with a solution to resolve it and complete it. Instead of thinking about it, resolve it in order to be more at peace. For problems that cannot be resolved it is important to accept the fact that it is unsolvable. In lieu of trying to anticipate the outcome of negative events or pondering possibilities with low probability you should be open to uncertainty. Do you think worrying will solve the problem or alter it? The answer is probably "no." It's not going to keep you from unpleasant surprises. You have to be willing to accept that the world is constantly changing. Finding the positive within these changes will assist you in becoming happier and less stressed.

In the Moment in the Moment

Being present in the present moment will aid in stopping worrying. The majority of times, anxiety is the result from the past, or the future. We aren't usually concerned over the things we're doing now. It is essential to let go of the past and be free of regrets. Every error is a learning experience, and each problem will strengthen you. The future is uncertain and the best option is to do your best to make the future you desire. It's not easy to do when you're worried!

It is important to learn how to appreciate the present or you'll never be able to be able to enjoy life. If you don't, you'll always want to be in the past, or be hopeful of an easier life in the near future. Tomorrow will never come, however. It's always today. Therefore you need to learn the significance of living in the present. Concentrate on the moment. Keep in mind all the positive aspects of today. To accomplish this, you might need switch off your gadgets and take a moment to appreciate the world around you. Pause for a moment to consider how wonderful the present moment is and become more aware. Let your thoughts be in the present moment, and allow you to block out thoughts of the future or the past. Take note the senses. What are you observing, hearing and smelling? What are you feeling, sensing and tasting? Instead of focusing on multiple tasks you can take a moment to be grateful for what you're doing.

It is possible to appreciate the finest things in your life. Take note of the little things and also what you may had previously overlooked. There's more to life that is obvious. Even the smallest of aspects can make the biggest difference to your life's happiness. Be grateful for everything, even the most insignificant things in life.

It is possible to enjoy the moment by smiling and bringing joy to those around you. Keep smiling and laughing. This can increase your mood and allow you live your life to the fullest. Make others happy too. Doing little acts of generosity can make a difference. You'll be happy knowing that you have made an impact and had an objective. Take time to be grateful for everything you've got and make sure to aid others who might need assistance as well. Every now and then, take the time to think about all the things that you are grateful for. Be positive each day.

Spend a few minutes with your mind. You might want to do some meditation. You can also breathe and pay attention to your breathing. Pay attention to the way your body feels, and then take a moment to unwind. It is possible that you aren't able to enjoy your present because you're too busy. Make sure you check in with yourself on a regular basis in order to remind you to be with the present. You'll need to make an effort to be conscious of this initially, since it is common to think about the future or think about the past. When you be present in the moment and be present, you'll learn to be happy regardless of how you feel.

Put aside the "What-Ifs"

There are many possibilities for "what-ifs" which you could be faced with. If you are one who worries all the time, you're bound to think that the worst could take place. But, this mindset is not going to help you in any way. If you always believe in the worst, and then expect the worst, you'll lose the drive to go on. It will be like you feel there's nothing to do because you'll expect the worst to happen. Therefore, it is crucial for you to end this vicious cycle and view the world in a positive light. While it is essential that you be realistic about your expectations, you shouldn't always anticipate to be prepared for the worst.

There's a right compromise between having realistic goals and remaining positive. You shouldn't have all the time hopes high for everything. it's just not practical to set overly optimistic expectations as you'll feel constantly disappointed. But, you should not think of life as useless and believe that things can never go right. Even though you might believe the latter is the more likely scenario, you have to be prepared to accept that life is filled with both struggles and success. If you are focusing on only one of them, you're being in the wrong.

The lessons learned from mistakes and difficulties can help you learn something about you, other people as well as life all around. If your life wasn't filled with problems and challenges, then the times of joy aren't as good. It is important to embrace the bad along with the positive and acknowledge that both are going to occur. This will enable you to live a lifestyle which is less stressful and filled with more joy.

Everybody has "what-if" thoughts every now and then. It's normal and may assist in making decisions. However, they could affect your everyday life if they begin to disrupt your daily routine. If you are struggling to get through your daily routine due to being overly focused on the potential for negative thoughts, you have to alter your thinking concerning your worries. If you're unable to manage your thoughts you're in trouble.

To keep these thoughts in check You can try some strategies. One method is to note your thoughts as they arise. In this way you become more aware of what you think. You may discover that these thoughts do not have a rational basis behind them. It can help you understand what you're thinking and be able to understand the reasons you think this way. It is also important to act to address these thoughts. If there's a way to address the issue you're concerned about, take it. If not, you must discover ways for you to release the idea. Discuss it with someone else, write it down or think about it. It is also possible to consider a moment to think about what the idea is and how it makes you feel, as well as what you think about it. This will allow you have a more positive emotional reaction to it and help you to be more effective in resolving the problem. Also, you must become at ease with uncertainty and change. Accept that some things are going to remain unsolved until they happen, and worry can't alter the outcome.

Be More Acquainted with Yourself

Self-awareness can be a huge help. It can make it easier to comprehend your thoughts and feelings, and to feel more at ease with your thoughts. You will understand the reasons behind why you behave and think how you think. You will know your strengths and weaknesses. are. This will aid in understanding what drives you. You'll become more aware of your motivations and goals in your life. It will also assist you in understanding others better and enhance your communication abilities. In addition, by increasing your self-awareness you'll have a more balanced body and feel better about yourself and your feelings.

To be more self-aware it is necessary to put in the effort to start by becoming more aware. Every day, take a moment to reflect on the way you feel. Be aware of your current mood and their causes and the impact they have on your life. It is also possible to look back on the day in general. Did you complete the goals you set out to accomplish? In the event that not, why kept you back from achieving it? Make use of this opportunity to constructively critique yourself. Don't just berate you, or compare yourself with other people, or consider the ways you fell short. Instead, look at the factors that helped you and what didn't. It will be beneficial by allowing you to learn from your experience and take it into the next day. It's not going to be easy initially But if you're able to improve every day, you'll fare better. Don't compare yourself with what you were before. It is essential to always be improving, learning, and transforming to improve. It's a natural process to grow in your life, and it's crucial to take the time to keep doing this to become the best person you can be. Be sure to consider both how you can improve and also what you accomplished very well. It's crucial to remember your achievements and keep in mind that you're competent to achieve success.

You can ask your friends to assist you in a variety of ways. One option is to share about your feelings with someone whom you are comfortable with. This will help you communicate your feelings verbally. It is also possible to ask other people for their opinions, since they may be able to offer an opinion outside of your own. But, it must be considered healthy. You must trust the words of the other person and make sure that you consider every word they say as an opportunity to improve rather than as an assault on someone you are.

It's also crucial that you can note your goals and values. This will help you become more aware of the goals you're striving for. If you don't set goals to achieve, you'll be lacking direction and significance in your life. Know what is important for you, and the thing that provides you a sense that you are important. If you don't set goals, you will not be able reflect on the progress you've made towards realizing your objectives. In the end, you won't be aware of what you're accomplishing.

The stress of worrying can hold you from achieving your full potential. Instead of having fun, you'll be worried. It's important to focus to minimize the amount of worry you have to worry about. Along with feeling more relaxed as a result, you'll also feel less anxious and stressed. You'll feel like a weight has been lifted off your shoulders. It will be much easier for you to concentrate on the things that matter instead of focusing on the things that don't matter. You will be able to see more importance in your life and will be able to focus on the things that matter to you. While at work, you'll be more confident in completing the tasks you have to do. In your home, you'll be more connected to people who are around you. When you're traveling you'll be able to enjoy your day without getting overwhelmed by worries.

It's crucial to break the worry-based behavior There are several ways you can take to reduce it. But, it is important to be aware that it's going take effort to get rid of worrying. It is also essential to learn how to be present to enjoy the moment and be happier. The stopping of thinking about the "what-ifs" which you are thinking about can be very beneficial. The majority of them are unneeded and you'll feel more relaxed if you don't think about these thoughts. Also, you should become more aware to be less stressed.

Chapter 4: Relaxing Anxiety

Everyone is anxious every now and then. It is normal to feel anxious prior to speaking in front of other people or before an important meeting or for an interview or any other similar event. However, those who suffer from anxiety experience anxiety to the point that they are unable to function in their everyday life. Anxiety could hinder you from going with your normal routine. It may hinder you from wanting to leave the house, or getting up. You'll lose motivation or feel inadequate, and will be unhappy. But, there are a couple of ways to assist yourself and make the stress less overwhelming.

There are a variety of methods to ease anxiety. The result will become easier to manage and you'll feel better in the end. This will help you be in control once more. It's important to acknowledge anxiety. Knowing what triggers you, and the potential factors that cause anxiety can aid in the resolution of the issues you suffer from. It's possible that you don't even know what triggers your anxiety or why you are struggling with it at all. It's essential to be able to discern between the normal and abnormal. It is also possible to improve your mental well-being, which will reduce anxiety levels and enable you feel more relaxed and more secure emotionally. In addition, there are many strategies you can implement into your daily routine to assist you avoid anxiety in the near future.

Anxiety Relief

Anxiety can be a challenge. If it starts to interfere with your daily life it can lead to a myriad of problems and hinder you from living life to the fullest extent. While it is crucial to seek out the assistance of an experienced medical professional when you need it There are a variety of ways to help ease your anxiety by yourself. Try these methods before you seek the assistance of an expert. Simple modifications can make a significant improvement in your anxiety and you can aid in feeling more relaxed. There are some options you can consider to ease your anxiety.

One approach to reduce anxiety is to take good care about your body health. Your physical health has a an indirect and direct relationship to your mental well-being. When your body's performing more effectively and your brain is functioning better, it is likely to function better. It will be possible to regulate your hormones better by taking good care of yourself, and your thoughts and emotions will be more balanced. By taking care of your physical health can aid in reducing anxiety, too. There will be less stress. If you look after yourself, you'll feel more confident about your abilities and more confident to achieve your goals. You'll not be worried about your health, and you'll be able to feel comfortable in the knowledge that you are taking proper care of yourself. Furthermore, you won't be concerned more about what others consider your appearance. You'll be happier with your self and won't be like you're as unsecure as you did.

A time of relaxation can help ease anxiety. Find the things that help you feel more calm and then incorporate it into your routine. For some, it could be a stroll in the park. You could also relax in the tub while reading or reading a book. Perhaps you have a passion that allows you to unwind. Whatever it is, make sure you include some form of rest into your schedule. Every day should include time to sit down, concentrate and unwind. Meditation can bring immense benefits since it calms the mind and leaves those who meditate with a feeling of peace. It is simple and inexpensive to do and there are a variety of guided meditations that are available both online and in person. If you're not a fan of practice meditation, taking a little time to breathe deeply will help you settle to relax and feel more at ease. This will help you become more conscious of your body and shift your attention away from the world around you focussing on you. Deep and slow breathing will ease anxiety. Certain scents can alleviate anxiety. Essential oils like grapefruit, lavender and sage may be added to baths in the house, or in diffusers to enhance your comfort and ease anxiety to a greater extent. The process of reducing anxiety doesn't have to be difficult or costly. Simple things like taking good care of yourself and giving yourself the time to relax can make a big difference on anxiety levels and will benefit you.

Healthy Habits to Prevent Anxiety

You can also incorporate healthy habits into your lifestyle to reduce anxiety. These are simple habits and can allow you to have a better mood and live an active and healthy life. Apart from spending time with yourself each day and letting yourself relax it is possible to incorporate the following practices into your routine which include taking proper care of your physical well-being. They can also improve your anxiety levels.

One thing you can include into your routine is exercise. If you prefer to train at the gym go on an exercise bike, run or swim, or even play sports, exercise is beneficial. It helps you keep your body moving. You'll feel better and it's the best method of taking care of your body. It will also allow you achieve a better feeling of overall wellbeing and to be more relaxed. It's a fantastic method to get rid of negative thoughts and provide you with something you can look forward to each day, particularly if select an activity you enjoy.

Another crucial practice is eating a balanced diet every day. Monitoring your diet can have a major impact on your overall health. If you feed your body with nutritious food choices the body will thank you by feeling healthier. You'll feel rejuvenated and more focused to complete whatever goals you put your mind to. Your body's metabolism is driven by the foods you put into it therefore make sure you're putting the right food items in your body for the highest performance that you can.

In addition, you must drink the correct drinks. Drinking enough water throughout the day is crucial to ensure you remain hydrated and getting the best quality of life you are able to. Consider adding an iced Chamomile tea in your routine as it is renowned for its relaxing effects on the body. It is recommended to avoid drinks that contain sugar since they only provide you with a short burst of energy, followed by an "crash," where you are drained and demotivated. Also, caffeine should be avoided as it can have a negative impact on people who suffer from anxiety. If you suffer from anxiety, it's important to pay attention to calming your body. Caffeine has an opposite effect on you. Also, it's recommended to stay clear of alcohol because it has similar effects.

It is also important to sleep in a healthy way every night. That means you must be getting the right amounts of sleeping. It is also beneficial to adhere to a sleeping schedule since it helps your body adjust to sleeping and rising simultaneously. For those who suffer from anxiety, it can be difficult in falling to sleep. To ease this issue you should not use electronics until an hour before going to bed. It's possible to develop a nightly routine, like reading, showering and relaxing for an hour prior to the time you go to bed. This can put you into the best mood to fall asleep and inform your body for rest. You should ensure that your bedroom is also conducive to sleeping. It should be peaceful comfortable, cool, and cozy. Put your phone down or in a different area, and ensure that your bedroom is dark. This will allow you rest better.

Recognizing Anxiety

Recognizing anxiety is essential. It will help you determine whether you have to improve your self-esteem and make some changes. You might not be aware the impact your anxiety has on you. an enormous impact on your life and it might even prompt you to seek out the assistance from others or yourself. It's also possible to recognize anxiety so you can identify whether you're experiencing anxiety-related symptoms and determine what the reason for the anxiety wave. It can be extremely beneficial to be able to identify the signs that you're experiencing anxiety.

While it's normal to feel anxious at times but there is a distinction between being anxious every once in the course of time and having to deal with anxiety. Although you might experience signs of anxiety prior to an occasion, in a situation that causes you to be nervous or when you take an action but anxiety goes beyond the sum of those. It is a continuous cycle of anxiety and worry. It can cause you to feel intense fear as a result of your daily routine. Every person is unique and the surges of anxiety are unpredictable and inexplicably uncontrollable. You can determine the triggers that cause anxiety and then work to avoid these people, situations and locations to be less stressed.

People who are suffering from anxiety may experience numerous symptoms and indications of their anxiety. It could be feelings of anxiety, tension, restlessness or increased heart rate sweating, hyperventilating and shaking. You may also experience fatigue, inability to focus and sleep or rest, stomach problems or a general feeling of a sense of dread. There are a few plausible reasons to feel anxious. As an example, it is possible that you might be anxious prior to an interview. You'd like get the attention of the prospective employer, secure the job and earn more money. It's normal and many are feeling the same. But, what happens when you notice these symptoms appear "out out of thin air." If there's no reason to believe that it's the cause, you could be struggling with anxiety.

It is important to know the root of your anxiety since it is unique for each person. Anxiety may be caused by various factors that include the past trauma or stress, personality issues or mental health issues the genetics of your family, drugs or alcohol. There may be an explanation that is specific to your. For example, people with social anxiety have a difficult time to lead a normal social lives without feeling a lot of anxiety. They might not be comfortable with strangers or in situations where they have to engage with other people. While it's normal to feel nervous when speaking to people at first, it can become challenging when you try to avoid any social gatherings and are unable to leave your home because of anxiety of having to interact with others. It is important to determine the cause for your anxieties is, so you can either conquer this anxiety or avoid situations that cause anxiety.

Enhancing your mental health

Improve your overall mental health can significantly reduce anxiety. You'll be able to concentrate better, enjoy more control over your emotions, and will feel less overwhelmed. The health of your mind is as crucial (if not more so) as the physical condition. If you're not able to maintain the right mindset and motivation, it will be difficult to care for yourself. Because of this, you need to take action that will improve the quality of your well-being and keep it in the best condition it can be.

One method to improve your mental well-being is by making an effort to improve your mental health. Take a look at yourself and say things that are positive. If you are able to see things in your world and events that happen positively, you'll think more positively about them. Find the positive in any situation, and remember what you're grateful for. You can tell yourself something positive that occurred every single day. Instead of focusing solely on the mistakes, failures, and negative things that happen every day life, consider and feel the joy all around you. It may take some time to master this skill however, If you make an effort to concentrate on positive things around you then you'll be in a position to do this in your subconscious. Be aware of the little things.

often, the smallest of details can make the biggest difference.

Make sure you are aware of your Present. You might get bored with repeating the same routine day after day or miss the value of an activity that seems irrelevant. But, you should be aware of the sights of smells, tastes emotions and sounds that surround you. This keeps you focussed on the present moment and lessen the need to worry. It's a great method to return to the present instead of being caught up on your mind. You could, for instance, just shower every single day. But, when was the last time that you actually enjoyed taking a bath? Pause for a moment and take a deep breath as the water hydrates your body. It is possible to spend a few minutes to thoroughly wash your hair and feel the soothing sensation of it. Consider how wonderful it feels to feel fresh and clean. Being grateful for the small aspects of life could make a difference.

If you are feeling overwhelmed or stressed, you need to do something to address it. Do not ignore the signals your body is transmitting to you. It's fine to take a break when you feel overwhelmed. While you might feel like you're removing yourself from the work and achieving less, you're actually doing yourself the right thing. If you push beyond the point at which your body is healthy and you are causing harm to yourself and become demotivated and unfocused. Walk around or talk to someone and write down your thoughts or simply breathe.

Anxiety can be a challenge to deal with and can have a profound impact on your daily routine. While everyone suffers from some kind or anxiety at times time, it's crucial to be aware of the signs that anxiety is more than simply being anxious about an important occasion or feeling hesitant about taking on a new challenge. If anxiety is extreme, it can hinder your ability to function effectively and hamper your ability to perform at a high level. It can cause you to go down and hinder you from living your life to its highest degree.

This is why it is vital to look after your self when you suffer or are struggling with any type of anxiety that you could suffer from.

It is important to ease your anxiety the best way you can. It's not difficult and you can test several quick strategies to ease your anxiety. It is also possible to incorporate healthy routines into your day to ease your anxiety. It's crucial that you're aware of anxiety. It is important to recognize when you experience anxiety issues and in what degree you experience. It is also crucial to know whether you're experiencing anxiety-like symptoms to be able to discern the messages your body and mind try to tell you. Understanding how to spot anxiety will help to identify the root of your anxiety as well as what might be triggering it. It is also important to ensure your overall mental health. This will allow you to feel more relaxed and also assist to reduce anxiety.

Chapter 5: The Superiority Complex and Self-Doubt

Everybody, eventually, doubts their capabilities. While it may be difficult it's normal for you might be wondering if you perform as well as others. It's also normal to feel a little inadequate for not performing as you had hoped or having the same level of confidence as other people.

However, the feelings of feeling inadequate and unsecure are meant to be sporadic or a matter of circumstance. If they occur they can cause you to think about them for a few minutes and then get on with your day by reminding yourself of your other strengths. If a significant event creates self-doubt you should discover ways to feel safe active, productive, and engaged.

It's often more difficult to do for those with the feeling of having an inferiority disorder. It is a term used in the past for persistent low self-esteem. Individuals with an inferiority disorder do not recover with the same speed. You might be able to complain about your flaws or make fun of yourself and criticize yourself in a harsh way in a bid to undermine your self-esteem, especially when it is at its lowest. The cycle may become so old that it is able to hold you back in your professional and personal life.

Self-esteem sufferers tend to be disappointed due to the fact that they have a low expectation of what they can expect. This becomes a self-fulfilling saga and as the disappointments pile up they make you more vulnerable and discouraged and you begin to feel a negative view of yourself. As a result, you perpetuate the feeling of being less than' in various aspects of life : physically as well as intellectually, psychologically and socially.

The positive side is that there are steps that you could do in order to cope with negative emotions and get over the psychological trauma that can be preventing your being optimistic. There are methods to boost confidence in yourself. Before we look at the options, let's talk about the concept of inferiority is:

The way Inferiority Complex Presents

Being confident that Usain Bolt will beat you in a race is not the same thing as feeling less than. A sense of inferiority is the unrelenting belief that you must perform in the same way as everybody else. It's not rooted in reality since all you can think about is that you don't have the same level of success, yet you are unable to pinpoint the reason.

The inferiority complex, also known as low self-esteem, is a feeling of inadequateness whose root is not rational thought.

The following list is of feelings that people who have self-esteem issues commonly have to endure:

The feeling of hopelessness and despair are crucial emotions for anyone who suffers from depression as well. It is a feeling that, regardless of how hard you try you will never be as successful as you could be or what other people seem to be. No matter how well you perform, it isn't good enough. It is normal for top performers to think that they are not good enough.

Anxiety - In this situation you are afraid of being exposed or being discovered to be insufficient. You may also experience the feeling of being insecure even when you're performing well in various aspects of your life.

Resentment as well as defensiveness and jealousy - You may experience anger, jealousy and defensiveness in such a way that you're unable distinguish them. They can be accompanied by guilt.

The friend I have, Caroline, often said she was 'ugly. In reality she wasn't, however, it didn't have any significance. Being ugly and feeling ugly is a different thing. In this state mentality, proof of reality of other people is usually discarded and rationalized away. It must be done to ensure because the self-esteem complex shields itself.

Caroline is then continuing to practice the story that she believes she is not adequate enough. She is soon unable to express her feelings clearly, even as she attempts to explain her feelings and explain where they stem from. What is the place where you believe her insecurity was born?

Consider this scenario while you read the remainder of the chapter. Try to answer the question at the conclusion based on the information you have learned.

The history of an inferiority complex

The APA (American Psychological Association) defines the term "inferiority complex' to mean the fundamental feeling of anxiety and unworthiness that one experiences due to physical or mental inadequacies.

The phrase was coined in 1907 by the influential psychoanalyst Alfred Adler. Adler used it to explain the reasons why so many people don't possess the drive to act most beneficial to them and to achieve the goals they set in life.

Psychologists, psychiatrists, or mental health experts employ the word as a synonym for low self-esteem.

Signs and symptoms of inferiority complex

As we've mentioned before it is normal to feel inadequate at times However, the real issue lies in the way you react to the emotions.

Do feelings of inadequacy encourage you to improve and learn? They ought to. Are they causing you to lose your temper and become distrustful? Or, do you become angry with others and blame them to feel better? Do you blame others for situations that you can change? If patterns such as these appear to be consistent across a range of circumstances you could develop an inferiority complex.

It is an assortment of negative emotions and thoughts, as well as tendencies and behavior. There are a few indicators to be aware of:

Perfectionism

In this scenario it is normal to overcompensate to compensate for what causes them to feel unworthy. Someone could strive to do better and excel in all they accomplish. Sometimes, they can become arrogant when they talk about their accomplishments to the point that they appear like they are narcissists.

You would rather fade to the background

The inferiority complex is closely tied to avoidance behavior. In other words, you don't feel at ease with being ignored or you are hesitant to step into social situations since you are scared of being disregarded. It can get to the point where other people are aware of your discomfort with your self.

Sensitivity to criticism

Self-esteem sufferers are extremely susceptible to the opinions of others and can be a target for resentment even if they are not intending to. Any form of criticism or criticism is held and discussed. They are not disposed to jokes or jokes at their expense. When they feel unwelcome by others, they use the aggression of others in order to intimidate them, and minimize the fear of being victimized.

Fault finding

If you're self-esteem is low and self-esteem, you could make the habit of pointing out flaws in others. You are more critical of others. If you see a friend who appears to have more success than you and you are able to be sceptical about their path to success instead of being content for them. Some take it to the next level, threatening others and constantly putting them down.

You will only be liked in the way you shine above other people

Human nature is prone to comparison however there are healthy and safe ways to deal with it. The best way to deal with it is to concentrate on being an improved person. If you are suffering from an inner sense of inferiority and you are focused on being more superior than other people.

Don't believe the words of other people's praises

If you are self-conscious the comments of others about your strengths are not true. It's important to remember that the most common issues with self-esteem stem from the early years of family relationships and childhood This will be addressed in the next chapter on managing relationships.

You think that the worst is true too quickly.

Being optimistic is defined as being prone to seeing the worst aspect of things , or thinking that the worst could occur. If you have noticed that you dismiss people with the tiniest of excuses It could be an indication that you've got problems to resolve. For instance, if your partner cancels a date for dinner however, they provide a valid reason, you might not agree to go on a new date because you believe they're not interested in you. If people stop too quickly, they are suffering from an inferiority complex and could be leaving out of the whims of their own ego.

Other indicators can include:

Continuously focusing on the upsetting thoughts

The decision to withdraw from friends, family members and friends

Refraining from speaking out due to guilt, shame, embarrassment and helplessness

Accepting responsibility for the mistakes and mistakes of others

Looking for attention or validation through fake depression, sickness or even illness

Avoiding any competitions where efforts could be in comparison

A sense of inadequacy is not just a problem for you, but can affect the people who surround you. The good thing is that you don't need to be a slave to it.

Risk Factors and the Causes of Inferiority Complex

Before implementing corrective measures before implementing corrective actions, it is important to identify the root of the issue to ensure that it can be dealt with appropriately.

Studies suggest that behavioral and psychological traits that contribute to low self-esteem are rooted in the following causes:

Genetics

Genetic research has revealed that some people have variations in the receptors of the hormone oxytocin that is that is responsible for positive emotions. Certain variations can result in people feeling less positive and suffer from lower self-esteem, as well as poor self-esteem and low confidence in themselves.

Family-friendly environment

Early caregivers can have a major impact on how your genes for self-doubt have been tempered or made worse. If a parent is extremely critical might take their opinions and continue to carry their negative attitudes to adulthood. As a child it is the time when you are most susceptible to being influenced. If you are constantly criticized and criticism, there is a good chance that you'll begin to feel weak, powerless and unsecure. The legendary Greek philosopher Aristotle once wrote, "Give me a child until he's 7 and I'll reveal who I am."

Society

There are unrealistic expectations everywhere including social media advertising, to authority figures and famous people that can quickly reinforce your perceptions of yourself and lead to self-doubt. Everyday, society bombards you with advice about how to conduct yourself how to dress, what you need at a certain age, what size of your body that is ideal as well as the type of hair you must have and the kind of automobile that are perfect. The messages can be subliminal. While you aren't aware you may be absorbing those messages and become your internal critics. You begin to feel devalued until you believe that you're not worthy.

The most common characteristic among the spectrum of people who suffer from low self-esteem is the fact that they compare them to others in negative ways. In an environment where you are always be told to purchase items because of their worth as you are fed an ideal diet and perfection, it's not difficult for the self-esteem issue to get worse. It is said that it's what's in the innermost part that is important most. But, our society is focused on celebrating someone's fame or wealth, car or body weight superficially.

The thing that makes it more difficult is the fact that people be able to say one thing and then do something else, and when you are feeling less than others because you're less, you succumb to self-pity instead of working to make yourself better. The shame only exacerbates the issue.

One of the most important aspects of embracing a positive attitude involves knowing the right time to turn away from the lies. It's about self-awareness in looking at your shortcomings and striving towards their improvement. It's not about using your imperfections to define oneself like Caroline in the example above did. It's not about hating self-love. It's about cultivating self-love, being supportive as well as encouraging your self.

What are you going to do with your inferiority disorder?

The process of dealing with an inferiority is a complex

Face the emotional traumas

In most cases, if you suffer from an inferiority complex, you will experience numerous negative feelings that cause you to think. Through this process, look at your thoughts. It is possible to practice journaling using prompts that will help you broaden your perspective and test your thinking. Sometimes, you draw conclusions from an emotionally charged incident that isn't true in the entire spectrum of similar situations. For example, a distraught woman may think the men in all situations are gamers but in reality each situation is different and the next man she meets could be the one she dreams of. Journaling can help you unravel situations and gain an understanding of them.

If you feel strongly It is best to confront them directly. When you do this the same, your thoughts will get more manageable and calm.

In a practice, you should zero into the sensation you feel most often that you would rather not have for any reason. You can close your eyes, and think about the feeling. If it triggers a specific memories where the emotion was shared, then that's an experience you must sort through.

Be aware that it might be difficult to complete this exercise at first instances, but once you get through it the effort, the weight of the experience diminishes and the memories continue to become less painful. This exercise can be done with someone whom you trust, but be sure to inform them on the process prior to starting.

Be yourself

In the lines that were spoken by Oscar Wilde, 'Be yourself and everyone else is gone' (1890). The most important option you have in life is to acknowledge the person you are and work to be the most perfect version of yourself you can.

When you cease worrying about what other people think of you is the moment you're completely liberated. One of the main reasons that afflict people is the desire to be similar to and be as someone else. This is to let go of the things that make you different. You can't impersonate someone else and remain true to your own self. It's not going to be a pleasure to recreate the life of someone else. That's not to say that you can't learn from others or get the same role models.

In reality, having others influence you, it means you can incorporate some of the traits that they exhibit into your own. However, it doesn't mean that you'd like to live in the same way that they lead. The self-defeating mind will flourish in the event that you try to portray somebody else.

Be specific

Sometimes all you need to do is to acknowledge the thing which makes you feel inadequate. What do you feel like you are lacking?

It is common for emotional thinking to blow things out of the realm of. Being specific can help you determine if your thoughts are not in line with logic. You can ask yourself questions which will aid in identifying your thoughts. For instance, out of all the people around the world who make you feel less than? What is the reason?

It is possible that you feel afraid of wealthy individuals, academics attractive people, well-known people. Then, continue to zoom into your surroundings and discover if you're too picky in the people you select to judge yourself against.

Live your life in a different way

"The only dare you wish to take is to become everything you are." Catherine Pulsifer

The majority of people are enslaved to the opinions of other people. They are afraid to be who they are. It's not as strict as it was where the only options that a person could choose from were those available in their village or town. With the advancement of technological advancements, options for career opportunities have expanded. Remote workers are now working with employers they've never had the pleasure of meeting. You can dress your hair shorter or longer and be considered trendy, not being a snob. What is considered to be appropriate formal dress has been altered. Traditional norms have been tossed aside. Today, you have greater freedoms than ever before.

The most important question to be asking yourself is what do you wish to accomplish? Don't be concerned if it's not in the norm, and do not be tied to what you believe you're supposed to do.

Eliminate the utopian notions

A lot of times that you feel less than, you're relying on the all-or-nothing mindset. Utopianism involves regret and a fantasy reality. It's about the 'if only' ...' thought' that continually go through our heads. Many people make the error of thinking they'd be happier if that they looked more appealing or made more money or had more that they could have.

It's not always that way. It's possible that you'll feel more confident after losing 20 pounds. But, what causes people to feel less confident is usually more than just a matter of ego, and reaching the desired goal might not satisfy the requirements. This could leave you looking for more. The objective is to be satisfied and grateful as an individual.

Everyone has deep needs. We want for love, connect, to contribute and to develop. These desires must be fulfilled to lead the life you want to live.

Summary

The chapter focused on the inferiority complicated and its place against an optimistic mindset. You learned about what low self-esteem is like and how it manifests itself as well as the risks and the reasons and how to handle the issue.

When the inferiority complex comes to the fore, it is a smack in the face:

Be specific about your feelings to help you understand them.

Eliminate the notion of utopianism

Face the emotional traumas

Be yourself and be yourself.

Make a choice to live differently!

Chapter 6: The Habits, Rituals, and Daily Habits, Rituals & Daily

Habit: Why is Important?

In the realm of positive self-talk and positive thinking, the importance of habit is paramount. When we develop a habit of something, we create the habit into a routine. The habit of routine, as you'll be able to see is crucial as well as essential in the process of making the switch towards healthy self-talk and a long-lasting positive outlook.

As negative self-talk is conditioned by repeated stories and beliefsthat get ingrained over time, the habits have positive benefits (or ought to be). When they are repeated enough and incorporated the habits are absorbed into your unconscious. Your entire self is embodied by them, making them the standard. This is the main distinction between habits that you have adopted as well as conscious rituals and daily routines: habits are a natural part of you.

It is possible to retrain our minds and, consequently, incorporate daily routines that allow us to live life in a state of positive energy being calm and focused whenever a real challenge or conflict arises, and drawing beautiful scenarios and situations to our daily lives. If we don't have routine and habits in time practices that brought us so much satisfaction, happiness and peace of mind are lost and were forgotten. Habitual practices reinforce those that seek to fulfill our highest purpose and helps us stay in a state of memory. The phrase "one step forward three steps back" is an excellent way to remember in this case.

In the following chapters, we'll look at various techniques, methods and exercises necessary for positive self-talk and positive thinking. If you are tempted to wander off the path, think about how crucial routine and habit are. Remind yourself (remind that you need to rewire your mind!) of the feelings, memories and experiences you had as your most positive, loving serene, peaceful, and joyful self. Your habits will transform into a mentality and a manner of living.

Rituals and Daily Prays

Like routines, rituals, and routines are repetitions of something that you want to keep ingrained and remain committed to. They could be exercises or mantras, daily thoughts patterns or any other habit that helps you stay in a state of remembrance. In contrast to habits, which are things that you forget about over some time, rituals are something which you create a conscious as well as conscious attempt to adhere to. They are regularly practiced and are a regular aspect of your daily life.

Let's take a look at some rituals we have in the present. A lot of people around the globe engage in daily rituals to help them reach a desired goal, path or even enlightenment (to reveal something) We can learn from them. Here are a few examples.

Awakening with a cup of morning coffee. Coffee early in the day is an habit that becomes a routine after it has been accepted and incorporated as a regular part of the daily routine. This is also true for those who have switched to lemon water in the morning green tea, honey-infused green tea and superfood-based smoothies! These rituals for morning are not uncommon.

The steps to follow after working or on days off. Many people have routines and routines to conduct their lives when they've reached a rhythm within their lives. For example, after work, cook the kettle, take an evening shower, curl up with a good book or read, cook the meal and take care of your plants, etc. Rituals don't just apply to the things "out out there" however, they are also used in the everyday, mundane routine.

Spiritual and Shamanic rituals. Many people choose to follow an esoteric ritual like burning incense, doing mantras every day and focusing on mindfulness through music therapy in the morning and taking time to sit and meditate before going to going to bed. These rituals have a targeted purpose and are generally beneficial to an individual's mental, emotional and spiritual wellbeing and overall health. Rituals that are based on Shamanism (any routine that connects to the earth and natural objects like crystals and spirits) can help us learn a lot. Though they might appear to be a little "woo," they are really based on a high degree of commitment, dedication and discipline towards an ideal goal and purpose.

Ceremonial ceremonies. When looking into rituals, it's important to be aware of the significance of ritual ceremonies as they could be seen as a ritual at its most profound expression. This is the time to learn about the quantum, energetic, and metaphysical aspects of reality as well as our connection to the world and attempt to carry out cyclic actions to keep us conscious and at the forefront of unison consciousness. When we talk about"cyclic," we're referring to weekly, daily or monthly events including rituals that align with the full and new moons as well as eclipses, equinoxes and solstices. A majority of people are aware our connection to nature and are therefore able to perform rituals to improve their emotions, mind and spiritual wellbeing in the way that they can. These kinds of rituals can include the setting of intention and manifestation as well as healing and sound therapy, moon circles, journeying as well as conscious sharing and circle of poetry, as well as connecting with the nature.

The Force of Gratitude

The power of gratitude is a effective thing. When we feel, think and show gratitude, we are attracted. Everything that you can see of is composed of energy vibrating, vibrations and subatomic particles interfering with each other. Every physical thing is affected from our thinking, emotions and energy-based desires. Being in a state of gratitude or even actively saying thank you whenever needed, will help in your personal growth.

If we are grateful for some thing or person is a way to improve the quality of the thing we are grateful for. It works on the fundamental frequency and law of attraction basis. Your thoughts and intentions ripple out, and even though we don't actually see the change (though it is likely that, in the majority of cases it's there) it is happening and changing cells at a deeper level. This is because gratitude changes the wiring of the brain. How does this happen? It can happen diverse!

First of all, it is crucial to remember that gratitude has to be sincere and genuine for you to be able to experience its power. Saying thank you without any substance, depth or emotion is not enough to convey that power that we are talking about in this article. The force of gratitude is an energy current that is transmitted to the person who receives your gratitude is able to pick up on. Since life is about being happy, feeling good and joyful and living in a state of harmony is when the frequency of your happiness and joy gets amplified. This is why you attract the positive experiences that you find yourself grateful for into your daily life. New neurological structures and synapses within the brain are formed when you practice gratitude regularly and is integrated into a system of having a positive outlook on life.

Exercise: Start to incorporate gratitude into daily life. Take note of all the things in your life that enriches your life in some way. For example: the bed that offers you rest along with your friends and family and the sun that makes you feel positive and brings you joy and the flower that is a reflection of your own beauty and the food you consume and everything else. Be sure to thank people in a way that is genuine, emotional and simplicity. You'll be amazed at how happier and more joyful your life is.

Another method that is especially efficient for increasing your gratitude and encouraging positive thoughts or thoughts and experiences to you is to incorporate the mantra of gratitude into your daily routine. The study of mantras is in the last part of the chapter. So make sure you refer to "The The Power of Gratitude" and then apply the meaning and purpose for your mantras!

The power of Journaling

Similar to gratitude, journaling is especially effective in helping to improve positive self-talk and positive thinking and improving all aspects of life. When we write, you are able to let out our feelings. When we write we heal and let go, and once we are healed and let go and let go of those "stuff" that holds us back. In letting go of the things that are no longer serving our well, whether it's thoughts, beliefs, memories or even traumas and wounds by actively creating space for the fresh to come into existence. Journaling is offering ourselves the space to be accepted, a sense of belonging, and freedom to express and, ultimately will only be positive! Even if you begin (or is continued) with a large amount of negative release, keep in mind that this is also positive. Like the myth we discussed earlier that being positive doesn't erase or minimize the shadow. These dark and unfavorable elements of life continue to exist. By journaling, you are able to release these and look into what they might be.

Journaling becomes an opportunity to learn and is an exercise in self-evaluation. Soul-searching is essential to the path to living a happy and peaceful life with confidence and control, as the memories, emotions experience, memories, and even our personal worlds are able to be examined. The emotions, feelings and personal wounds are usually hidden within our souls, and it's only through reflection, such as journaling, that we bring them up to surface. You might discover that your unconscious repressed traumas or memories can be triggering your beliefs that are limiting or negative experiences, or you might be surprised to discover that journaling can trigger memories that you didn't think about. It will then bring happiness and bring back memories of something that could make your life pleasant!

These are only one of many examples. It is important to keep in mind that journaling lets you fully be you by exploring a wide range of memories, emotions of stories, thoughts frequency, and other aspects of your conscious as well as sub-conscious mind, which has shaped you and your life's path. Journaling can be a way to develop positive self-talk. A self-talk written on paper.

Exercise: Purchase a special journaling book. Take the time to to reflect and let your thoughts and thoughts wander, allowing any thoughts that come to mind. It is also possible to focus on any subject that brings an awareness of self-development, learning and healing. Over time, you will realize that this journal will become your bible of sorts and result in a variety of positive interactions and experiences.

Exercise 2: Start a dream diary! Dream diaries, or journals are basically records of your desires. They can serve as a sort of guide for life since dreams can provide insights into the various aspects of your life. There are often signals, messages, clues and direct insight in our dreams. And numerous people around the world have been able to tap into their dreams in a conscious manner. Lucid dreaming, astral projection and interpretation of dreams are just a few examples of these. Journaling about your dreams and recollecting them can help you to examine your shadow, hidden emotions , emotions about a situation. memories you've forgotten, as well as possible future scenarios.

The power of Meditation and Mindfulness

Meditation and mindfulness could be among the top two potent ways to begin or to expand and develop as you transition to positive self-talk and positive thinking as a approach to living. It is possible to even write a book on the subject since it's an extremely rich field to explore. But let's begin by introducing the basics.

To meditate means to reflect. When we sit down to meditate it is like filling our minds and body with the space of the creation. Everything physical arises from space and quantum physicists have discovered that each atom is 99.9 percent empty space. The universe as well as everything that is in it is essentially unformed! Physical reality therefore is only a tiny percentage of the energy that is the basis of it.

Through meditation it is possible to replenish ourselves with the necessary space to improve our thoughts, mind, and ways of being and observing. Mind, we all know is an instrument. It is a tool that shapes, creates and influences physical reality through the thoughts, emotions, and perceptions it creates. Meditation and letting the mind to relax can increase awareness, which allows all kinds of positive outcomes to occur.

Let's examine some of the benefits of meditation in the context of its own. (This list isn't exclusive!)

Enhanced cognitive capabilities

Increased mental clarity

Focus and concentration are increased.

Peace of mind

Inner peace

Ability to tackle problems without difficulty

Positive outlook

Greater awareness

A boost in intuition

The perception of subtle energy and spiritual aspects of the human experience

"Genius" mentality

Innovative, artistic and imaginative advances

Greater compassionateness, empathy and care and compassion

A feeling of love for all as well as oneness and unity

Health and psychological

Mental spiritual, emotional and physical health

Self-healing capabilities are enhanced for a variety of physical illnesses

Vitality and energy are more abundant.

It sparked interest and passion in the world of

Enhanced cognitive functioning and a willingness to new knowledge and participating in projects or studies that are unique.

More intimacy as well as connection and interaction

Communication and speech enhancement

Better understanding of other people

Improved sexual health and vitality

More law of attraction, and manifestation capabilities

Longevity

More power to fight diseases

The destruction of cells that are unhealthy

Releasing, healing and letting go emotional issues

Better ability to face any struggle, hardship, or obstacle

A change in one's whole manner of being

Alongside these benefits Meditation also improves the capacity to develop mindfulness. How can mindfulness be defined?

Mindfulness is the deliberate practice of being aware. It's being aware and keeping focused attention regarding any aspect, topic or aspect of your life that needs to be explored. For instance, you could meditate on your appreciation and gratitude for nuts or your favourite food that gives life force to increase the effectiveness of this subject. It is possible to meditate on confidence in order to boost the level of confidence (a quality) and also contemplate in a mindful way any circumstance or memory to gain understanding, wisdom and understanding to aid with any aspect of your life (or to improve the quality of your life). The basic idea is that mindful meditation is a practice that can have many different results.

In addition to mindfulness meditation, there's also mindfulness which involves engaged participation and involvement with your daily activities. For example, a walk through your favourite park could transform into a practice that is mindful by paying attention to your attention and directing your mind to a particular topic or thought trail. You can make an effort to pay attention to the different kinds of birds that sing, and tune into their tunes to bring peace or a sense of being connected with the universe. It is possible to be aware of your thoughts as well as be aware of the emotions thoughts, emotions, and sensations which arise from any outside observation. Mindfulness comes in a variety of kinds, but the basic principle is that you're consciously increasing your awareness of your daily life by following the direction by which you think.

Of course, this also impacts your ability to be positive in your thinking! Like meditation, when you improve your mindfulness, you are changing your brain (and the neurons inside) to feel, perceive and think, act, and behave in a different way, often in a way that is more in line to higher ideals. What are the ways that the higher values be manifested? Joy, peace, happiness connections feelings of intimacy and the love of wisdom, love, compassion as well as empathy, sight increased awareness and cognitive function confidence and inner knowledge intuition, as well as enhanced psychic abilities are just some of the things that can be enhanced by focusing on mindfulness.

Let's examine some of the specific kinds of meditation and mindfulness, and the ways they can be utilized to enhance self-talk and positive thinking.

Meditation in silence

The practice of silent meditation helps in quieting the mind to create an effect that is desired. As you will see from the above list the benefits of meditation are numerous and therefore it is not necessary to go through them again here. The main benefit of meditation that is silent is that you fill your body with space, allowing the cells of your body and your inner systems like the immune system, as well as the brain's neurons the space needed to heal. Meditation is a method of healing because you concentrate on your breathing and permitting a better circulation of chi, oxygen, and energy. More oxygenation of cells is a result, leading to a variety of positive results.

Since all thoughts originate in space, breathing air and quieting the mind can allow for more awareness to grow. This increased awareness can lead to positive self-talk and positive thinking.

Meditation for the mind

Meditation that is mindful is one that is conducted with an intention, goal or the focus. The focus is typically on the subject you would like to "be aware" about, for example, building confidence, compassion or self-esteem. Meditation is a great way to be utilized to treat any wounds, traumas or discomforts that are weighing you back. This is because mindfulness can get to the core of the issue and can be utilized to investigate various aspects of one's self. In essence, anything and everywhere you choose to focus your attention can be focused. The mind is the spotlight shining on any goal you would like to shine light on. This can, in turn, assist in self-talk that is positive and improve certain traits associated with.

For instance, you could contemplate confidence, energy or happiness. It is also possible to meditate on compassion or intuition, or even emotional intelligence. The trick is to become connected to the quality and embodying the way that it manifests. Begin by focusing your attention on the mental or visual representation of the quality, and then contemplate the energy it brings with the quality, how it feels, as well as memories of conversations, events, or moments that you've experienced in that state. Once you've created a clear solid image that is attuned to the experience of it all of its components, the main thing in mindfulness is surrendering into the feeling and let it in. This allows the awareness and space to fill your body and improve the quality within your. In this way you are creating the possibility of a bridge between you and what you want to improve. Of of course making the decision to make it a part of positive thoughts is what generates an entirely new sense of self-talk. This is a powerful thing!

Chapter 7: The Effects of a negative mindset on your Quality of Life

A negative attitude can impact your health in profound ways as you've learned from the last chapter. It can also impact your general quality of life. If someone has negative thoughts and is depressed, their self-esteem, their professional life as well as relationships are affected too.

In this chapter, we'll be looking at the various impacts that a negative attitude can affect the quality of your life. Understanding the effects is crucial to be able to see how an unhappiness with your life could be the root of many issues.

Low Self-Esteem

The dictionary says that self-esteem refers to "confidence in one's self-worth or capabilities." Many people employ self-esteem in conjunction with self-worth and self-respect. In simple terms, self-esteem can be one of the most important factors in determining one's success. Don't assume that having lots of self-esteem is a guarantee that you will be successful more quickly.

The reality is that you must have an adequate and healthy self-esteem to yield positive results for yourself. Many times, those who are not confident in their self-esteem are more likely to be depressed or engage in self-destructive behaviors. They may fall to make poor choices or result in relationships that are unhealthy.

People who don't take pride in their thoughts and opinions are likely to be self-defeating. They tend to not focus on their strengths or the recognition they merit instead, they focus on their mistakes in the past and perceived weakness. They often have the perception that other people are more competent or superior than them.

They also struggle to accept positive feedback. They are afraid of failing, which stops them from doing things, and eventually hinders their progress.

Below is a list of the symptoms that are displayed by the case of a person with low self-esteem. Make sure to tick off the ones you believe you display. If more than four boxes have been checked then you're likely to feel low self-esteem.

You are doubtful about your abilities to achieve success.

*You chose the wrong partner for you.

You criticize people frequently.

* You're scared of being on your own.

* You become stiff.

You always place the needs of people around you above your own needs.

*You often feel ashamed.

*You are afflicted with anxiety on a regular basis.

*You often feel depressed.

The Effects of Your Professional Life

If someone has an unhappiness with their mind can cause lots of anxiety and stress in their work environment. Deadlines seem to be a lot tighter and work is less valuable. If a person is unhappy with their job, anxiety rises and work becomes more stressful. This results in more stress. It's a vicious circle. Let's examine the stressors that may result from being in a negative state of mind.

Career Crises

A crisis in your career could be being denied the job you've been hoping for or feeling that the job you're in isn't in line with your ambitions and goals. This could result in a massive change in your mood at work. This could result in anxiety getting to work, since you might feel that you're wasting your time doing nothing in it. Because you're at work for the majority of your time even if you are not completely being unhappy at work can affect people's health, which can lead to anxiety when you go back to work which makes you feel miserable.

Financial Woes

As the price of life is rising up in the major cities, people are frequently finding that their pay isn't enough. Finding it difficult financially and stressing over which bill they're paying for first is a major source of anxiety in the lives of people. Furthermore, the employment market isn't exactly flourishing, so getting a job that pays higher wages isn't a viable alternative for the majority of people. There are times when they may experience anxiety or concerns about how they'll get by and this can be a nagging thought that lingers in their minds and then turns into anxiety. The anxiety can trigger negative thoughts about their work probably due to feeling that their efforts aren't adequately compensated.

Work that is not fulfilling

Work that is not fulfilling is frequently discussed in terms of how it encourages negative feelings. For instance, even though doctors may be in a more stressful and stressful job, they might feel satisfaction or joy by helping others and making a difference in the lives of others. This is what may keep the doctor going through difficult times. However, those who have an occupation in sales may experience an excessive amount of stress due to the demands placed on them. However, they may not get satisfaction from their job.

When someone is extremely overwhelmed and unhappy They begin to experience anxiety about their happiness. This then it turns in anxiety about their lives and their work. This is why people frequently make a decision to cut their pay and quit a stressful and not fulfilling job to take on a job that pays less, but can be more fulfilling or less stress-inducing.

Once you've mastered the primary reasons for stress at work it's crucial to be aware of the signs and symptoms. If you suspect that you're experiencing workplace anxiety examine yourself and determine whether you're displaying any of the following signs:

*Feeling irritable

*Trouble sleeping

*Avoiding family/friends

* Over/under-eating

*Feeling down

*Tiredness

*Mistakes in memory

*Muscle tension

*Loss of the interest you have in your work

*Difficulties with Concentration

*An ambition to be the best

Feeling like you're going "crazy"

* Constantly worried

*Crying

Fear of making mistakes that is unfounded.

Influences on Your Relationships

Negativity in relationships can cause many difficulties. The relationship is not only less likely to succeed however, other crucial aspects such as sexual relations are affected as well. The negative effects of negativity can cause an anxiety-producing situation for the couple as well as anxiety is shown to adversely affect someone's sexuality. Let's examine the negative consequences of anxiety and negative thoughts on the sex lives of people.

It is not just that negativity can hold you back in your work and cause stress for you , but the fear, anxiety and anxiety that go along with it can cause anxiety in your sex lives too. According to research in the sex and relationships area, all anxiety and negative thoughts can be a hindrance in the pursuit of sexual fulfillment. Let's discuss how anxiety affects various aspects of your sexual life:

A negative mind lowers libido

Anxiety and feelings of depression can affect your sexual drive in a variety of ways. The feeling of overwhelming that you feel during episodes of anxiety may take over your thoughts and force any thoughts about sexuality out of your mind and hinders you from getting into the mood, even though you felt it earlier in the day.

The emotions of worry and anxiety can have a significant physical impact on your body, as they increase levels of hormones that cause stress (e.g. adrenaline) which can cause you to feel uncomfortable or tense. If you're experiencing difficulty in relaxing your body and experiencing sexual sensations, and even achieving orgasm is extremely challenging.

A negative mind lowers body confidence

Being naked in front of someone else can be a stressful experience for the majority of people. Even if you've been naked in front of someone many times before! But, if you're experiencing anxiety, you're more likely to be anxious and self-conscious. You may also be obsessed with your "body imperfections."

Like women and men and both genders, they can both be extremely self-conscious about their body's shape, appearance or body component. When you feel uneasy or depressed this self-consciousness increases.

If people constantly feel criticizing themselves for self-shaming They shut off their ability to experience sexual pleasure. They also have a difficult time being emotionally active and physical during sexual sex.

Negativity causes struggles with intimacy

When someone is overwhelmed by anxiety and fear and anxiety, they might not wish to be physically or emotionally with anyone, not even their spouse. If you've had a trauma from the past sexual contact, sexual intimacy or even sex can cause anxiety and be frightening.

If someone is affected by the recollection of previous incidents or negative experiences this can trigger the system to shut off completely and stop any sexual experience from being enjoyable enough to warrant an emotional climax. If the person doesn't recognize this, they might begin to stay away from sexual activity or any form of play, which could create tension in the relationship.

Negativity causes difficulty in consuming gas.

Anxiety is often accompanied by symptoms that include a shallow breathing pattern and tight muscles. They can play a significant role in keeping an individual from letting go and experiencing an orgasm. Anxiety-related symptoms can increase the threshold of an individual's "orgasmic. The word 'orgasmic threshold' refers to the length of time and amount of stimulation an individual needs to experience an orgasm.

When the patient is woman, anxiety could stop the body from producing the necessary lubrication, which makes their body uncomfortable. It can also trigger vaginismus. It is the disorder that makes the vaginal muscles very tight to the point that it is impossible to penetrate.

These kinds of physical changes coupled with anxiety and a negative mindset can affect the person's perception to sexual stimuli.

Chapter 8: Think It

If you've realized that you tend to lean toward negative thinking, you're not the only one. Life isn't easy and it can take its effect on the most positive person. It requires a lot of self-awareness and discipline to alter negative thinking however it can be altered.

It is impossible to control the motives of other people or their words or their reactions to situations however you do have total control of the motives behind the words you use and the way you respond to situations. The way you respond to a situation could completely alter the situation positive or negative. the worse. If you have confidence in yourself and recognize the situation for what it really is, your response is not likely to be detrimental to the scenario.

With confidence in your self-image and confidence in who you really are, you are able to keep your cool regardless of the situation. Secure people

They create an uplifting vibe that others can see that and are able to trust them. They don't emit a positive vibe. confident or arrogant individuals, I'm talking about confidant humble, simple people who are confident in their own personas and are the type of person you would like to be.

When other people can feel this peace and strength that you possess and feel secure within you. If you are always taking the highest way and act in the right way, you'll create an aura of security around you. Honesty, dignity,

being calm and having the ability to discern what is actually happening will safeguard your.

One of my routines every at night, before falling asleep, is run through the HADS. What is the HADS? I'm glad you were curious. Here are my HADs

H: Did I cause any harm to anyone?

A: Was I upset or rude with someone today?

D Did I do anything dishonest or rude to anyone?

S: Did I show selfishness toward anyone else today?

The easiest and most efficient method to develop positive is to alter the way we communicate with people who surround us. This will not only aid in developing positive attitudes, but it also helps strengthen your relationships with other people and bring greater joy into your lives.

When I review my HADS, I take mental notes of any interactions I had with my spouse, my children as well as my coworkers, and that lady at the drive-through I think everyone. If I realize that I've violated one of my HADS, I take the initiative to rectify it when I next see the person. I apologize sincere for my conduct, without making an excuse for my actions or words. If you can make just one change in your life to greater happiness, this is the thing you must make. Even if you don't do anything in the book If you implement this one thing, I can assure to you your relationship will be transformed to the better.

The next thing I do following my HADS is to run through my entire day in my mind. What I mean by that is that I go through my thoughts the day before and then I evaluate

Their impact on my day and impact on my day and. I attempt to identify those thoughts that are negative or negative that may not be truthful and then counter these thoughts with at minimum 3 positive thoughts about the topic. I then engage in a bit of role-playing in my head on how to resolve the issue or resolve the issue or accomplish this goal without any negative thoughts.

Many times, after having done this, I discovered that I had missed an opportunity to move my life or situation in a positive direction. The way I see it is that I begin to think about this idea for a few seconds before evaluating the amount of effort and time it would be required to achieve this goal. Based on the speed at which I could accomplish it I then decide to either move ahead or to dismiss the idea. If something seemed to be too difficult I'd be tempted to give up and belief that I couldn't accomplish it as it would require too long to accomplish compared to the rewards. When I re-examined the thought at night when I have a fresh outlook, I am able to accomplish it in less timeand for an even greater reward.

There are times when you'll be trying to make a choice regarding something. It's not because you

Rejecting an idea or thought because it is a bad idea doesn't mean you were thinking negatively. If you've done your homework on that thought or thought as not the most appropriate option, then stay to that.

It wasn't necessary to have an unfavorable opinion.

If your opinion about something was self-defeating, or demeaning toward yourself or your idea then you must conduct an into consideration the implications of this.

If you can accomplish these two things just before you go to sleep, it will drastically alter your perspective on life, the mood you have throughout your day and eventually your life's success. When you get there, you'll be able do this in the course of the day as it is taking place. If you can accomplish this, you're on the way to making your day more positive by thinking.

It is important to note also positive thinking isn't just wishful thinking. Thinking positively is method to look at things in a different way and interpreting things with a clear view of what they actually are. It removes all thoughts that are negative, and "dark" thoughts about things. Negative thinking or dark thinking is generally not the norm.

Real or accurate. Place your thoughts in the light and everything will become clear.

If you can look at things from the perspective of positive thinking , then you're in the right position to take the next stage of being successful, being confident in your own abilities.

Chapter 9: Loving

If you had the option of choosing victory over failure, then you would not select failure!

It is an endless series of decisions. There is no need to compromise in order to choose one decision over the other. You can make your choice freely since it's your choice.

What you feel about your dream is love. The strength of love is the most powerful thing we have and when we love, it leads to actions. Love is the source of strength. Keep the love in your heart and never give up on your goals. Always go for love! If you choose to live with the love of your heart the path ahead will be easy.

In the end, aren't we not all one species on our tiny planet? Space views will make this clear because we don't be able to discern race, we will not be able to discern gender, nor judge by either language or beliefs. We have a significant element that is in our collective hand in the idea of unity. In unity, there is love.

Your success is based on the long journey to the top and you need to be accountable to yourself as well as to other people. The destination you will reach is likely to require strong relationships and alliances. This is only possible through unity. The force of unity is among the strongest in all the Universe. Without it, there's nothing but chaos.

As you progress each day toward your goals, you should remember to create relationships, and not burn them. Do not rely on individuals, instead join them. Allies and alliances are crucial to get to the highest levels.

You might not be aware of it, however your attitude towards positive thinking and how you nurture it can have significant impact on your overall well-being. Additionally, keeping your brain filled with positive energy can affect the way you interact to those in your life.

Additionally, having a positive outlook will help you come up with solutions for the challenges of daily life and also solutions to issues that always arise in the business world. In addition, it can assist in understanding the perspective of the people around you and sustaining a sense of unwavering respect for those around you. This is an essential element to the building blocks of business development. Also, odds are likely that you'll require these aspects in the process of achieving your goals and dreams.

Your improved self-image will also benefit your romantic relationships. Your ability to discern the benefits of a different perspective can help you build emotional intimacy.

In this way, the increased empathy you feel for your spouse will be useful in the event of miscommunications or the escape of a word you've thought was lost or not intended.

We've all experienced how difficult to be around people who has a negative or gloomy perspective can be. We make the choice, whether we do so voluntarily or unintentionally to surround ourselves with those who are enthusiastic and encouraging. The reason is that the company of this kind of person is incredibly energizing and enjoyable. If you are a positive person family members and coworkers will enjoy being in your presence, and that is how great companies emerge.

Positive thinkers are also more likely to be more focused on resolving problems instead of creating or worrying about the issues. Studies have shown that people who are positive thinkers are more able to manage tension and conflict in a manner that's practical and efficient. Offering solutions to problems will always help to resolve the issue and clear the path to take regardless of whether it is in the context of business or personal matters.

Many of us believe that positive thinking may seem like the ideal solution to our issues and as the best solution to eliminate negative thoughts. Positive thinking is viewed as something that's gentle and to idealistic, but is actually practical, just like persistence and determination. But, perceptions of these terms are rapidly changing because more studies are being conducted. Psychologists are showing that positive thinking goes beyond than simply faking a positive mental state to convince yourself that there is nothing incorrect. Positive thinking can bring real benefit to life by helping develop and enhance your abilities and combat the negative consequences of stress.

There are many instances of this. One example is of the cougar leaping ahead of you when you walk through the desert. Your brain's first reaction could be terror. Since your brain has been trained to have a certain reaction to this type of emotion Your "instinct" could be to flee, without considering other aspects. The only thing you are thinking about is your fear and ways to minimize it, and on running away from the coyotes. This negative thinking can affect how you respond to the situation. The best choice is to climb a tree to grab items to make a weapon from, or simply to remain at peace and hope that the animal doesn't see your presence. Instead, you'll be running with the knowledge that the cougar will beat you.

This could be a helpful sense of instinct, and it could be logical to think this it is, considering that you're unlikely to meet an elusive cougar in the city. The main thing you can learn out of it is you're not making decisions based on the issues that you're facing. Your mind is making choices based on your negative thoughts, with no consideration of any other variables or alternatives.

When you're in an disagreement with someone else the negative emotions that you feel are anger and anger and. It can cloud your judgment and may cause you to make statements that you do not intend to say. Similar to this feeling overwhelmed in the beginning of a long day at work could affect your performance and be as severe as making you feel numb and preventing you from beginning any task. Being negative about your body may make you reluctant to exercise and can cause you to feel as if you're unmotivated regardless of how much motivation you may actually possess.

In all of these situations the brain ceases thinking about your surroundings and the aspects it must consider and instead focuses on your negative thoughts similar to what that it was in the case of the cougar. These negative feelings keep you from thinking out of your box and from considering ways to be more effective and from making sound decisions. Instincts aren't good but it's better to make the effort to think through all the information you have and then take action accordingly.

What positive thoughts affect your brain?

If you are experiencing positive thoughts and emotions you brain release endorphins which could trigger you to feel additional positive emotions. You might begin feeling happiness, joy, contentment even affection. These feelings will then open your mind to broader positive and more positive thoughts. But, this is just the beginning. Positive thinking could have greater impact in the future.

Develop your positive thinking skills

Although positive emotions and feelings are beneficial, even if they are experienced for only a short duration, they aren't the only benefits from positive thought. The real benefit comes from these feelings that is the capacity to learn and enhance your skills that you can later apply to various aspects of your daily life.

For instance, consider the happy child. The child would go out and play with their buddies play, run around and participate on physical games with them. The child becomes more athletic and agile. They also acquire social and communication skills much faster than a child who is unhappy. The games can also inspire children to be more curious about the world around them. Simply by feeling satisfied and acting on this emotion, a child will develop physical, social, and imaginative skills.

It is possible that emotions won't last for long time, but the skills they possess are. An athlete will be strong and healthy and may be eligible for the opportunity to receive a college scholarship to play a sport that they love and excel in. A child who is social will have a much easier interaction with their superiors and peers and could earn promotions faster. Children who are creative can come up with creative ways to express themselves through art, resulting in more positive thinking.

Negative emotions can do exactly the opposite. They block individuals and the acquisition of new skills. They force them to focus on their current issues, but they do not assist them in finding solutions.

However, if positive thinking is able to aid in so many aspects of our lives How can you be more positive?

Enhancing your positive thinking attitude

What can you do to improve your positive thinking skills and to enhance your abilities?

If you're reading this, you have an idea of what makes you feel happy. It could be a pastime or relationship, or even a goal. It could be that is as simple as listening to your favorite music. Anything that brings joy to you will help you feel more positive.

Three things you can do to also bring joy to your life:

1. Meditation People who meditate tend to show more positive emotions than those who do not in research. People who meditate can develop and improve their capabilities.

A sense of mindfulness and meaning in life are both things you can attain by meditative practice, as well as the improvement of your immunity.

2. Writing writing about positive experiences can improve your mood. An analysis of two groups of students, one of whom wrote about their experiences over three months and the other who didn't, confirmed this.

The first class of students benefited not just from an improved mood, but also from better health, as evidenced by fewer trips to the doctor.

3. Play: Set aside time during the day for playing. Similar to how you schedule appointments and meetings in your calendar, plan play time Make it a priority and adhere to it.

You can make use of the hour to make something, or to enjoy yourself in any way you wish. Consider the last time you enjoyed yourself and not feeling that it was preventing you from doing things more productively. When you make it an important priority and then make time for it, it's less of a hassle and becomes a normal element of your daily routine.

Don't waste this time to sit back and relax on the Internet. Make time to watch your favorite TV show, talk to someone you haven't spoken for a while or perhaps create something new. You can feel joy and positive emotions by doing things that truly make you content, rather than things that only satisfy you.

Happiness and. Success

Happiness is the result of any accomplishment like being promoted, advancing in an affair or winning a competition. The achievement of a goal you have decided to achieve will definitely bring joy, happiness and happiness. However, success alone isn't always a guarantee of happiness.

We think often, "if I get this one thing, I'll be done and never need anything other than this."

We can also imagine, "Once I achieve this I'll be satisfied and will not need to strive higher."

It is important not to depend on your happiness to the goal you've made for yourself. Instead, focus on increasing your happiness today to build and develop the abilities which will enable you to achieve your objectives.

At the end of the day, your success may not always bring joy, but happiness can be the key to success.

This is a fact that is proven through studies. People who are content tend to make progress within their life. Their happiness allows them to learn new and useful abilities that later can be utilized in their path to success. The success brings happiness and the cycle repeats.

What can we do next?

Positive thinking isn't an undefined term used to make people feel happy about themselves. Being happy is great but it's also essential to develop and build the abilities you require to succeed whether in your work as a teacher, in your education or even in your private life.

Happiness is more than bring feelings of happiness for a short time and reduce your stress levels. Making choices that bring you joy for example, taking part in a game or learning something you enjoy, will help your wellbeing.

Moments when you feel happy are the moments where you can be positive and think about ways to use your experience to help your future as well as how you can improve your skills that will help you in the future career or ways to inspire yourself to take your career to the next level.

For the sake of this, Be positive, seek happiness spend time doing things that bring you joy. Success will come naturally.

Many people classify the feelings they feel for love within the course of a relationship as addiction and you've probably been there too. It's actually true. Studies have shown that the chemical processes the brain experiences when it falls in love is exactly the same as that which occurs during addiction.

"Love is a mental state that is part of our genes, and influenced by our childhood. We're wired for romance due to the fact that we are expected to be loving parents who take care of our children who are helpless. The romance of love excites and inspires us. It is essential for the continued existence for our species. If we didn't have the romantic love, we'd reside in a different world that more closely to the social groups in our animal kingdom. The chemical signals that are circulating inside our brains when we're feeling love have multiple functions, and the most important objective is to ensure the survival of our species. These chemicals makes us want to create families and to have children. After having children, those chemicals shift to make us want to stay with each other to raise the children. In a way the love we feel is actually an addiction to chemical substances that is created in order to continue reproducing."

The love of romance is an integral aspect of life for anyone regardless of their culture and surroundings. The culture may produce various ways to show love, but the fundamental love remains.

What is it that makes us be in love?

Every person has the "type." That's the set of traits we seek in a potential partner. it's the way we distinguish between someone we would like to establish an affair with, and one we wouldn't. There are many variables that are at play when it comes to our personality.

Appearance:

Researchers have discovered that we are inclined to be drawn to people who are physically like our parents. However, others have observed that we may prefer people that look like us.

Personality:

Similar to our appearance We also are attracted to those with personalities which remind us of a parent or those whom we were with in our youth, simply due to the fact that they're familiar.

Pheromones:

Pheromones continue to be an important issue when it comes to love. The term "pheromone" originates by the Greek words "pherein" and "hormone," which translate to "excitement carrier." We can see the presence of pheromones within animals in the form of scents within their body fluids. These images show their sexual activity and attracted by animals of opposite gender for mating. The organ inside the nose of an animal, known as the vomeronasal detects hormones.

The existence of pheromones has always been debated, along with their role in influencing sexual attraction.

For instance sea urchins release pheromones into the water, signalling to urchins that are in the colony to let them know they are ready for a mate and causing their mates to "eject their sexual cells." While this is a simple process for animals, it is not the case for us.

In the course of your lifetime, you may have felt sweat on your brows and a slight twitch in your belly, a warm smile on your face, and an explosion of emotion as you first laid eyes on your lover and then realized that the initially "love on first glance" sensation actually is due to a chemical signal that is initiated from the brain.

According to numerous research studies "love is at first glance," or the act of gazing at someone you're incredibly drawn to for the first time stimulates your brain to produce three different chemicals: dopamine Oxytocin, and opioids. These are the substances that can make you fall in love.

Researchers have devoted their careers to investigating the chemical processes of love falling into love and what the brain goes through when we experience love and passion. Dopamine has been proven to be the strongest chemical involved in the process which can trigger feelings of joy, excitement and excitement.

Chapter 10: Take proper care of your body

A healthy body is the best method to be a better person and to feel more comfortable with oneself and to build self-confidence to relax tensions, and improve the ability to apply the principles for positive thoughts and optimism.

Mind and body are, in reality, inseparable units that are connected via two threads such that any issue in the emotional realm can be immediately manifested onto the body. Just as any issue in the body can have the ability to alter the mood, leading to depression and sadness.

It's not a coincidence that the old adage "Mens Sana in corpore sano (the body is healthier and the mind healthy when the body is healthy as well)" was coined in antiquity has won the approval of scientists through the years and is passed down to us, and is still accurate, wise and convincing.

Let's take a look at what is meant by taking charge of one's body in order to have the ability to attain an emotional state that is satisfying and is conducive to living in the spirit of optimism.

RESTRICTED RULES IN ACTUALITY

1.) A PERFECT LOOK Take care of your body from all angles can also mean improving your appearanceand making every effort to be successful. In the beginning, you have to adhere to strict hygiene guidelines, to ensure that you always appear fresh and smell fresh. Also, you must wear clothes that make you feel comfortable and elegant, i.e. that go perfectly with your personality and style of living. It's unwise, in the alternative giving yourself up to poor hygiene, giving your beautiful clothes, to maintain your appearance only in the context of a social event, and to follow the unhealthy fashion of dressing badly and not combing your hair when staying at home. This approach that is so typical, robs the vitality emotion that is triggered by feeling satisfied with your physical appearance. This charge, in reality is what makes one automatically able to think positive thoughts and take on the day in the most positive possible manner.

2.) Regularly practicing a physical activity: This is another essential rule to be adhered to. Moving can help reduce the tension, enhance the tone of your muscles, boost blood circulation, and reduce the calories that are absorbed by food. It also helps you to not gain excessive weight, which can be detrimental to your health and appearance. It is essential to make sure that the activity you select doesn't amount to a lot of effort or, even more importantly or, a boring effort. If the gym is dull and boring, then it's definitely worthwhile to change your routine and whether that is walking for long periods (preferably with a partner) at most four times a week, or a modern dance or a Zumba course that are both really enjoyable and extremely rejuvenating.

3.) Non-permanent important diets Don't continue to smother your palate by consuming sloppy and unhealthy diets, if you follow which you'll only experience the devastating consequence of weakening your body and depressing your emotions. Food is among life's best pleasures and to completely stop is a burden which is not one worthy of attempting, as it affects your psychic sphere in a negative way. To stay in check while you relish the pleasures of eating at the table, all you need to do is must get into the habit of eating meals and lunch with only one thing you love very much (for example, during lunch you should have you can only eat pasta and, at night, an ounce of ham or an alternative, a delicious piece or cake). This way you will achieve the double purpose of not having to give up the freedom to eat what you like while consuming a smaller amount of calories.

4.) AFFECTING LARGE IMPACT ON your sleep: Sleep shouldn't be sacrificed due to any reason. Because no moment is as vital to the body as well as the soul like a peaceful night's rest. This is why the legendary Canadian psychology expert Stanley Coren referred to "excess awakening" the most dreadful and harmful scourge of our time. Actually, our bodies and minds need at minimum nine hours of sleep each night to be efficient, yet most people do not pay attention and keep fighting and screaming about the necessity to sleep, dragging them into a series of routines that cast shadows on the following day. Nervousness, bad mood and constant tiredness and dizziness, as well as difficulty finding the positive side of different situations is in reality the cost you incur when you fall asleep extremely late.

5.) Respecting the strategies of the "GOOD NIGHT" It is important to adhere to the methods that will allow you to rest comfortably and get the most benefit from sleep. Don't sleep fast but don't head to bed right after having eaten too much food. Both situations create an organic state which prevents you from sleeping peacefully. Before you go to bed avoid the urge to sit and watch movies and read novels that are either too frightening or exciting to create the conditions for nightmares. The trick to fall asleep quickly when you're exhausted, anxious and stressed. Another way to get and energized is to try when you lie down the mental practice that will follow. The mind has to create a circle and "write" within there the numbers 100. Then, next to the number, think of "sleep" as a word "sleep." You can erase the number 100 , and then trace the number 99, constantly keeping your eyes on "sleep. "sleep." Remove it and mentally draw the numbers 98, 97 and the next. In the majority of cases you will fall asleep prior to you reach the 50th number.

Chapter 11: Establishing Fruitful Relationships

People who believe in the human condition assume that any relationship could be the source of bitterness, conflict or even humiliation, which can be disconcerting and emotionally unstable.

On the contrary, believe that having a good relationship with other people will always bring pleasure and allows them to grow to feel more comfortable and integrated throughout the world. The key to this belief however, which unfortunately is finding less and less support lies in a set of rules, which when created as their own, enable us to build productive authentic, full and real human connections.

Let's look at ways to be loved and loved, and form bonds that are fulfilling in all aspects.

REGULAR RULES

1.) Be well with yourself 1) BE SELF-CAREFUL: First it is crucial to realize that in order to truly love people and feel at ease with your friends who are family, friends or even relatives they are, it's vital to feel loved and comfortable about yourself. The first step towards creating relationships that are successful is to get started connecting, cuddling, and loving with one another. It's not as easy as it seems it is healthy selfishness that allows one to give oneself a hug whenever possible, means one puts the health of oneself first on the priority list and encourages people to constantly seek an advantage for oneself regardless of the situation, is the solid foundation of altruism and compassion for other people. It's no accident that someone has said: "Love your neighbor as you would love" and nothing more than you.

2.) Learn to always be yourself: The secret to being authentic is to concentrate not on the appearance of oneself instead, on the actions and actions, not wearing masks or acting in roles. As an example when speaking with someone, you must be attentive to what you say and what's said without noticing where you're sitting and not worrying about judging gestures or taking postures you find attractive. This way, you'll effortlessly develop the spontaneity that brings you tranquility as well as looking attractive in the eyes of your interlocutor.

3.) leaving their personal identity to other people: It is vital for others to be themselves, and not have the utterly absurd desire to alter them to create a similarity to the models they have created. The first thing to remember is that changing anyone else isn't possible and by engaging in this irrational idea with anyone, you will only take away from yourself the goal of your own goals to transform and risk losing, based on the circumstances it is the love of your spouse and the affection of your peers, and the affections of your teenagers. Everyone should be accepted as is who he is, and valued for the good qualities he has and if those good qualities aren't evident within him it indicates that there is a conflict which makes it necessary to break up the relationship.

4.) Avoid negative people: To eliminate without mercy from your life people who are negative that are always in a negative mood, pessimistic, eager to complain about a scandal and often filled with jealousy. It's not sensible to be around people who cause discontent, or frequently choose to engage in unpleasant topics of conversations, or those who are unsatisfied until the very end, as by doing this, one is at risk of falling into the vicious circle of suggestions. Additionally to that, believe it or not negative people also emit negative energy that can be a source of stress for many hours, if not even days. Particularly, it is essential to eliminate from one's life people who, under the pretense of honesty, feel forced to disclose any the evil that is bothering you. an honest friend, a person with whom you can truly build a positive relationship, will never report any wickedness due to the fact that he is not listening to it, or even nip it off if the incident occurs within his specific surroundings.

5.) Do not relapse into a cycle of anger This is another way to be open to other people and be able to feel at ease throughout the globe. Inability to forgive is in reality a problem of the emotional realm and is a poison that corrodes and drains lots of energy. Learning to forgive isn't simple, but it's important to confront this fatigue, not due to the misunderstood notion of "goodness" towards the bitter end, or to show respect to an unwise gesture of generosity towards people who have committed wrong, but to rid oneself of the dark ghost of resentment which is that is extremely uncomfortable and irritating. In the end forgiveness is a an essential part of loving each other.

6.) Always be sincere In all situations, sincerity and with any person you interact with is essential to be comfortable with people and to avoid being in the embarrassing and uncomfortable situation of not being able to remember the lies that one has made about oneself. Be careful, however, being sincere doesn't mean that you are rude. For example, telling an acquaintance "How old are you in the past year since I've seen you" isn't honesty however it is rude. Sincerity can be used as weapon to assert the needs of one's self and establish friendships that are loyal and unshadowed. For instance, sincerity could be saying to people who offer an invitation to dinner last moment: "I just can't tonight because I'd rather be with my son, whom I haven't seen for a while. There's nothing difficult about appearance, but many would prefer to turn down an invitation by saying ("I have no choice because I have work to complete") instead of being honest about it the person doesn't understand whythey are embarrassed. In doing this you block others from knowing who you are (you refuse to spend time with your son, and you claim to be more interested in work than having a night out with your buddies) and therefore make it difficult to establish more genuine and lasting relationships.

Chapter 12: How Thinking Positively can assist us in developing our abilities and enhancing our work performance. Enhancing Our Health

On the surface, Positive Thinking looks like an ideal idea, and many of us would rather have positive thoughts over negative ones any day. But the concept "Positive Thinking" is such an easy concept that many tend to ignore it. Our minds are engrossed in the notion of complexity and we're not drawn towards anything until you understand the complexity. We're taught to see the world in this way and in this world the phrase "Positive Thinking," which is a basic concept is swept in the shuffle. Actually, these concepts have the same significance like some of the words on the English Language, such as "Persistence" and "Work Ethic" do. While the perception about the universe is evolving, our society is beginning to accept the basic things that make us happy in this world.

Many studies have been conducted in this area Researchers have discovered that positive thinking goes beyond the feeling of being content or displaying an optimistic mindset. Positive thinking can result in a real costs to our lives, and aids to build a skill that lasts forever. The impact of positive thinking for our job, lives, and even our health has been investigated by numerous researchers. One of which are Barbara Fredrickson, whose study is further discussed in this article. Barbara Fredrickson works as a scientist on positively oriented psychology in the University of North Carolina and has published material that offers an interesting new perspective on positive thinking and how it impacts our capabilities.

2.1. What negative effects do we have on our brains:

In order to understand this, we need to make a scenario to explain the issue in full. Let's think about the situation in this way: we're walking along an alleyway, when suddenly muggers cross the street ahead of us. When confronted with the situation our brain is triggered to register the negative emotion which in this case is the emotion is fear. Researchers have proven repeatedly that negative feelings we experience trigger our brain to react in a specific way. For instance, when a criminal crosses the path of our vehicle, we immediately begin to run. The other people and its surroundings don't have any significance in this instance. Our attention is solely on the present situation and the emotions it creates within us, and how could we do break away from that particular circumstance. If we consider the situation from a subjective perspective negative emotions tend to limit our thinking and focus it to a specific area and focusing our minds on one thing that is negative. The brain is unable to see other possibilities available to us and focuses on the one that is the most vulnerable to negative emotions.

It is a great instinct to the fight or flight nature, however in our modern society, we don't need to be concerned about it. The problem lies from the brain. Since it is designed to be a negative emotions in every circumstance possible. Our brain shuts out the outside world and restricts the possibilities of being able to understand.

Let's look at the situation in this way: We are involved in a heated debate with someone else, and our emotions and anger are all over the place. those negative feelings that emanate all around us are eating away at our minds to the point that the fight is all we think about, and it takes the mental health of our loved ones. When we're so overwhelmed by all the tasks we need to accomplish for the day, it can make difficult to begin things, since we get rigid due to the size of our to-do checklist, and consequently are unable to complete anything and instead slumber in a state of negativity. There are a variety of situations where negative thoughts affect our brains human brains. We create these naive negative spaces within the minds of our brains that they drain off in a way that is so disconnected from reality. We lose motivation, and we get lazy and eventually, it affects our health.

In all of these situations our brain is shut out from the events of the world. It creates an imaginary bubble of negativity surrounding itself, focusing on negative energy and emotions such as anger, stress, and anxiety.

2.2. How do we affect our brains by positivity:

The long-standing problem of whether a glass of water is empty, or full, how can respond to this dilemma? This is a question that is grounded in psychology, and it defines our perceptions and outlook on life, how we feel about our own existence and whether we see life with optimism or in a negative way. It's also believed to impact our well-being. Numerous researchers have studied this particular study, and numerous studies reveal that these characteristics of our personality known as optimism and pessimism can affect various aspects of our health and wellbeing. Positive thinking associated with optimism plays an important role in the successful managing of stress. The effective management of stress can have numerous positive impacts on health. Therefore, there's nothing to worry about when you tend to lean toward negative thinking when confronted with the old question. However, we can develop positive thinking abilities.

Positive thinking isn't the idea of placing our heads in sand like an ostrich not focusing on the negative aspects of life. All these things are part of the daily experience and should be taken care of in a positive manner, like. Positive thinking implies that we approach every negative aspects of the world with positive perspective, which results in more positive outcomes. We shift our mindset to think that the best things will be the case and not necessarily the most negative.

Positive thinking, as it is said repeatedly, is through self-talking. It always begins there. Self-talking with ourselves happens constantly every day and they're the endless streams of thought and the unspoken thoughts coursing through our minds. They are there while we're standing in a line, when we're talking to someone else, or while we're on the subway. These endless thoughts are present everywhere and these thoughts are the ones that make us think about every thing we see, and often because of our human nature, they're negative. A lot of our self-talking sessions are based on logic and reason however, many originate from our own fears and misunderstandings that we build within our minds as a result of the lack of knowledge.

2.3. Positive thinking can be beneficial to our well-being:

Numerous studies are currently being conducted as well as the study of the impact of positive thoughts and a life outlook that is optimistic on our health. The majority of studies which have produced positive results from positive thoughts on health include:

Positive thinking has been proven to prolong the life span of the person.

Positive thinking can lead to a decrease in depression.

People are more likely to experience less stressed when they view the world with a positive perspective.

The positive effects of thinking positively have also been examined for diseases such as the common cold. it was discovered that those who practiced being positive had superior resistance to common cold than those who were confined to negativity.

Positive thinking is known to improve the physical and mental well-being people.

In addition to the common cold Positive thinking was proven to be effective for those with heart disease and a lower risk of death due to CVD was observed in optimistic people.

It's a powerful strategy for coping and has been scientifically confirmed that positive thinking aids us to deal with the pressures and difficulties of life more effectively.

Researchers aren't sure the reason why these health issues occur to those with positive attitudes. One theory that has been widely circulated is that those who are more significant and have a more optimistic attitude to life are able to handle more effectively stressful situations, and it reduces the detrimental adverse effects of stress on our body. A different theory suggests that those who have a positive outlook and live their lives with a positive outlook tend to live an improved lifestyle and take care of their bodies more frequently. These people have a healthier diet and gain more energy in their body and avoid behaviors like smoking or drinking, which could cause harm to their health.

2.4. Enhancing our Skills Set by Being Positive:

The best thing about positively thinking is the fact that it's not a brief, instantaneous positive feeling; the benefits of positive thinking last for a long time. The primary benefit that having positive thoughts is an increase in our capacity to build abilities and the development of assets that can be valuable in the future. Take it this way, as children, we would play outdoors, climbing treetops and played buddies inside our treehouses or in the playground, climbing on the monkey bars. This helped develop a physical ability that allowed us to be athletically active. Playing with other kids and the ability to communicate with them shaped the capacity for social skill within us, and also the drive to discover and explore our surroundings exploring the outdoors when we were children, shaped the ability to be creative inside our heads. These abilities that we didn't have any idea we had , were cultivated in our childhood through playing outdoors and spending time with children and having fun and having fun, morphed into positive feelings that led to the development of these skills, abilities that can be useful in daily life.

These abilities that were developed because of the positive feeling of joy we experienced as young adults last a lot longer. the joy of playing outdoors with your friends is gone however the abilities developed through it are present. The fundamentals of playing on treetops or climbing the monkey bars could result in us being awarded an athletic scholarship to go to college. Also, the skills we acquired when we were chatting with our friends could result in our entering into company or becoming a supervisor of a business. The excitement that brought about the positive feelings through which the skill set was developed is now a distant memory however the abilities that we acquired remain in our minds.

Fredrickson came up with the idea of the "broaden and construct" theory. The name comes from the belief that the positive emotions that we experience broaden our perspective of the possibilities our environment and help open your mind up to the possibility of a different one. This is what allows us to develop new abilities with the earlier ones that we have in our mind and build up resources that give us with value in other areas in our daily lives.

In the same way, the emotions we label as negative, can be the exact opposite of this belief. The world is a equilibrium of opposites, therefore it's only fair that if we have one theory that is based on positive thinking, there is another one that is exactly the opposite. Negative energy stifles this idea because the notion of developing abilities for the future is insignificant when there is an imminent threat ahead of us, like we have discussed in the past by comparing the case that of the mugger.

We've talked about all of the benefits of being to positivity and positive thinking, and the benefits it brings to our lives. However, the possibility arises in our heads that whether this positive attitude is helpful in the development of the core of our beings as well as in the development of the skills which will aid us in the near future. What can we do to achieve the level of optimism that makes us feel positive and not even realize that we're actually doing it?

2.5. Positively enhancing our lives:

What can we do to incorporate the idea that we can incorporate the concept of "broaden and grow" in our lives to create more positive energy and transform our thinking process to one that is optimistic? We've said that the idea to "Positive Thinking" is the easiest to understand. It can be stimulated by the smallest things aren't paid attention to in our daily lives. Just like anything that triggers in us a sense of happiness, feelings of happiness or a sense of happiness will bring positivity into our lives. We know ourselves best and are aware of what makes us smile more than others and we are aware of what motivates us. Maybe it's playing the instrument we love most or having time with our parents, or with someone that is truly special. Perhaps it's like a tiny garden, or as large as designing houses or even a new house. Whatever brings us joy and inspires us to be positive. However, certain things can trigger an optimistic mood in a large number of people, including;

2.5.1. Meditating:

A variety of studies have been conducted by scientists about the impact in meditation upon the development of positive emotions within our daily lives. It was discovered that those who make a habit of daily meditation tend to exhibit a greater levels of positive emotions contrasted to those who do not practice meditation. In the discussion prior to the lifelong set of skills the study found that those who meditated developed greater, more unique and useful skills in long-term. It was discovered that people who practiced meditation often experienced an increase in their levels of mindfulness. They also were more socially supportive and had a stronger reason for living and showed a reduction in the symptoms of disease.

2.5.2. Write:

Writing is a fantastic way to bring positive outlook on life. If we write about positive things that happen in our lives as well as about topics that reflect a positive perspectives about them, it is easy to are able to feel the experiences we write about. We can feel the positive energy radiating out as waves and entering our thoughts. Writing about the positive moments of our day-to-day lives, allows us to revisit them and results in a positive feedback loop. It was also discovered in an experiment that when people recorded the positive moments they had experienced for 3 consecutive days, they had higher levels of optimism as well as less mood swings, and also had fewer instances of illness that seemed random.

When we begin writing about a specific subject, we begin to give it power. And when we write about positive experiences in our lives, or answer the random topic of positive thinking, we are on the quest to create positive energy. Writing can create a circle of happiness that is unmatched and that's why writing is a powerful tool for achieving your goals. Law of Attraction also gives the importance of writing about what we wish to achieve. Since when we begin writing, we are on an expedition to find the fulfillment of what we wrote about.

2.5.3. Playing:

Our lives are planned out and we plan conferences, meetings, events to attend, obligations appointment, and calls, and other obligations in our day to every day lives. We plan these events to the point that we begin becoming a machine. If we are able to organize all these activities so why not plan to play for a while? Our calendars are full of these meetings and appointments that aren't allowing us to play, just to enjoy ourselves for a short time, and to allow ourselves the time to be happy?

The life of a person is all about discovering new experiences, yet, despite filling our lives to the brim and have no time for us. What makes the human brain have this tendency? We plan and plan, but we don't schedule a time for ourselves. Allowing ourselves to enjoy our life with joy, smiling and be happy with the little things that happen in our lives and, most importantly having fun with this incredible existence called life. When we begin enjoying being a part of the fun it creates an optimistic mood inside us. When we schedule the meetings we have, what if we schedule an hour of enjoyment and fun, exclusively for us.

Chapter 13: Tips for Practical Use to Encourage You to Think Positive

To carry out a positive attitude, we must create here a positive perspective. Dalai Lama

For as long as we're human, it's nearly impossible to cleanse our minds completely of negative thoughts and feelings. Every so often one of these negative thoughts may pop up in our minds, but with determination and consistent training, we can minimize the impact negative thoughts can have on our lives. These are tips for every day life to ensure that the engine of positive thoughts flowing through us.

Practice repeating positive affirmations to yourself

Similar to the idea of imaginative visualization, using phrases such as "I will achieve it", "I shall succeed", "All is well" and other self-motivating affirmations boost our confidence. When you are before the mirror, tell yourself that "Today will be a wonderful day". It might sound strange, but reminding yourself to focus on positive thoughts by using affirmations is among the most effective methods to keep your mind focused. Consider incorporating words that invoke the power of control, confidence and happiness throughout your day.

* Surround yourself with positive people

Keep inspirational and positive pictures or quotes in a place that you can view throughout the throughout the day. This could be a photograph of you being awarded an award from your high school, displayed on your desk at work or a quote that you love on the reverse of your bathroom door. It is possible to keep a photo of your spouse and daughter within your wallet. You can take your wallet out every day to look at the photo. A simple flower vase placed on your table will provide you with a bit of optimism.

I have this quote by Alphonse Karr on my refrigerator "We can be unhappy because rose bushes are thorny, or be happy because thorny bush are filled with roses." Inspiring yourself with positively-themed images and images can be like getting an extra dose of positive energy. Take a look today.

* Smile constantly

The benefits of smiling throughout the day are numerous to mention. A smile will make you feeling content and happy with your self. It also demonstrates to others even strangers that you're generous and eager to help. Have noticed that when you meet people with smiles people will try to greet you with smiles of welcoming and joy at seeing you? This is the effect of smiling. Eric Davis said; "It requires a lot of effort for you to become negative. It is a process that requires effort to master it. Smile is a painless process. I'd rather focus my energy having fun." Don't you?

*Reboot for a moment

Are you overwhelmed by your negative thoughts and feelings? This happens to the most optimistic people often. For a moment, lie down, shut your eyes, block out any emotion take a deep breath and try to control your feelings. Slowly close your eyes, and attempt to remember things that brought you immense satisfaction. It might be the day that you became a bride or accomplished your biggest task. Remember the amazing feeling you felt when you are in that moment, then remind yourself everything isn't so bad in the end. Rebooting for a moment can help us relax and help us tackle tricky issues with the utmost confidence that we can find.

*Move along with positive-minded individuals

If we're happy with it and/or not, we can be sure that the most powerful external influence on our lives is those we associate with. Friends and family members who are happy bring more positive stories and positive outlooks, as well as encouragement and help to replenish our reservoirs of happiness. Be careful not to spend all day with that acquaintance or neighbor who is a negative person in every situation. Be aware that thoughts can be infectious and if you are constantly in contact with people who are negative there is a good chance that you'll absorb a portion of their negative thoughts. Establish and maintain a relationship with people who are positive. It's very difficult to stay negative when everyone and everything in your life is positive.

List the things you are thankful for.

This is a mental practice that will lift you from the deepest depths of despair. At some point in their lives nearly everyone has gone through an era when they feel that he's not in control of what happens to him, and feels like they are at the shorter end of the stick. If you're in this kind of situation, get in a chair with a pen and paper and write down the things that you're grateful for in your life. List everything that is possible even the smallest they might appear.

It is possible that there are only a few things you are grateful for, But you'll be amazed by the abundance of positive things that happen in your life. This will make you be aware of the joy you receive from your work or relationships, family, achievements in the past and overall health.

Conclusion

I hope you've been capable of managing your depression and anger and also alleviate your anxiety and keep your panic under control. You ought to have been able remove any negative thinking from your brain and free your mind so that you can focus on what is important to you. In addition, you should be at peace with your sleep and remove anxiety attacks from your life. You'll be in a position to understand how cognitive-behavioral therapies can assist you reach the goals of investing in your health and improving your happiness. In addition, you'll be aware of the steps to develop a healthy attitude towards your emotions and found the way to feeling happy. Overall, you'll enjoy an enjoyable life, with more efficiency and mental stability. The anxiety you experience will decrease since you will are less worried about and more time to enjoy life.

It is the next stage to apply your knowledge and apply the lessons you have learned in real-world situations and apply those techniques to your daily life. You can learn something new about CBT in relation to how it could aid you. You should think about researching more information about it, and then signing up for therapy. It can truly help you improve your life. Get started working on ways to combat depression and anxiety. You could incorporate certain practices for them into your routine and this can be extremely beneficial to you. Be conscious of depression and anxiety and how they impact your daily life. It is also possible to begin setting goals. Take the time to think about what you want to accomplish in your daily life, establish the appropriate goals to achieve thesegoals, and make a commitment to working towards these goals. You are able to take control in your mind and get rid of any negative thoughts. Consider the way you think and what you are thinking about in order to become aware to your thought patterns. Also, begin to observe your behaviour and how you react to situations.

www.ingramcontent.com/pod-product-compliance
Lightning Source LLC
Chambersburg PA
CBHW071838080526
44589CB00012B/1044